# Fighting Fit For The Latter Days

Leisa Ebere

Copyright © 2020 Leisa Ebere

All rights reserved, including the right to reproduce this book, or portions thereof in any form. No part of this text may be reproduced, transmitted, downloaded, decompiled, reverse engineered, or stored, in any form or introduced into any information storage and retrieval system, in any form or by any means, whether electronic or mechanical without the express written permission of the author.

The views expressed in this work are solely those of the author and do not necessarily reflect the views of the publisher, and the publisher hereby disclaims any responsibility for them.

ISBN: 978-0-244-26127-6

PublishNation
www.publishnation.co.uk

# Introduction

There is an end time harvest being prepared by God and we, as the Body of Christ need to ensure that we are up to the mandate of bringing the lost into the Kingdom of God. But when we are held captive by the enemy from oppression and poor health, our usefulness is limited and our attention is distracted from God's purposes, which is most assuredly Satan's master plan. But God has provided healing strategies for His children by both supernatural and natural means, and He is desperate for His people to open their eyes of understanding so that they can understand His truth in these matters, and so that they can live in divine health and victory until their appointed time comes when they joyously join Him in heaven.

It is important that we understand, as God's people, the reason we are in this state, and what our legal rights are from a biblical perspective; so that as we walk in recovery towards divine health, we can walk in total authority under the power of the Holy Spirit and in the name of Jesus Christ, the Son of God. And to understand properly God's plan, we must go way back in the Garden of Eden when Adam and Eve first went against God's decrees concerning the Tree of Knowledge and listened to the Satan (the serpent.) This disobedience gave Satan full authority over the earth and all its' inhabitants. But God loved us so much, that He sent His only Son and when Jesus Christ died upon the Cross, it gave us as human beings, a way of escape; because when He sacrificed Himself for <u>every sickness, sorrow and sin of humankind, a new authority was</u>

established in the heavenlies for His creations made in His image. So now, if we as His children accept Him fully and completely; then Satan's power over our lives is legally broken or cancelled in Jesus's name, forevermore.

This is wonderful news and although most Christians accept this truth; and walk with some degree of victory, their bodies and souls are still horribly attacked by the enemy. So why is this and how can these Christians break free from Satan's targeted attacks upon their lives? Well, the simple truth is, that we must align ourselves with God's will in our body, soul, and spirit, and God has given me incredible rhema knowledge as to how to help you on this journey, in this book. Beloved, God's Word confirms the need for this alignment in: (1 Thessalonians 5:23), which says: "Now may the God of peace himself sanctify you completely, and may your whole spirit and soul and body be kept blameless at the coming of our Lord Jesus Christ."

At the start of your journey to becoming aligned in body, soul and spirit with God's purposes, I would like to share with you an exciting end time prophecy by Tommy Hicks, an anointed 20th century evangelist, and then I will outline in the following chapters, how to become "Fighting Fit for the Latter Days."

**Tommy Hicks, an evangelist, was used by the Lord in the great Argentine Revival.**

God gave him vision in 1961 of the end times, a vision of the giant end–time ministry. (This vision began July 25th, about 2:30 in the morning, in Winnipeg, Canada)

The vision came three times, exactly in detail, the morning of July 25th, 1961. I was so stirred and so moved by the revelation that this has changed my complete outlook upon the body of Christ, and upon the end–time ministry. The greatest thing that the church of Jesus Christ has ever been given, lies straight ahead. It is difficult to help men and women to realize the thing that God is trying to give to His people in the end–time. I do not think I fully realized nor could I understand the fullness of it until I read in the book of (Joel 2:23), Be glad then, ye children of Zion, and rejoice in the LORD your God: for he hath given you the former rain moderately, and he will cause to come down for you the rain, the former rain, and the latter rain in the first month.

It is not only going to rain the former and the latter rain, but He is going to give His people in these last days a double portion of the power of God. When this vision appeared to me: I suddenly found myself at a great height. I was looking down upon the earth, when suddenly the whole world came into view every nation, every kindred, every tongue came before my sight. From the east and the west; from the north and the south; I recognized the countries and cities that I had been in. I was almost in fear and trembling as I stood beholding the great sight before me. At that moment, when the world came into view, it began to lightning and thunder.

As the lightning flashed over the face of the earth, my eyes went downward – and I was facing the north. Suddenly I beheld what looked like a great giant. As I stared and looked at it, I was almost bewildered by the sight. The giant was gigantic. His feet seemed to reach to the North Pole and his head to the South Pole. His arms were stretched from sea to sea. I could not even begin to understand whether this was a mountain or whether this was a giant. As I watched, I suddenly beheld that it was a great giant. I could see he was struggling for life, to even live. His body was covered with debris from head to foot; and at times this great giant would move his body and act as though he would rise up. When he did, thousands of little creatures seemed to run away. Hideous looking creatures would run away from this giant and when he would become calm, they would come back.

All of a sudden, this great giant lifted one hand toward the heavens, and then he lifted his other hand. When he did, these creatures by the thousands seemed to flee away from this giant and go out into the night. Slowly this great giant began to rise – and as he did, his head and hands went into the clouds. As he arose to his feet, he seemed to have cleansed himself from the debris and filth that was upon him, and he began to raise his hands into the heavens as though praising the Lord. As he raised his hands, they went even unto the clouds.

Suddenly, every cloud became silver; the most beautiful silver that I have ever known. As I watched the phenomenon, it was so great, I could not even begin to understand what it all meant, I was so stirred as I watched it. I cried unto the Lord and I said, "Oh, Lord, what is the meaning of this?" And it felt as if I was actually in the Spirit, and I could feel the presence of the Lord, even as I was asleep.

From those clouds, suddenly there came great drops of liquid light raining down upon this mighty giant. Slowly, slowly, this giant began to melt – began to sink, as it were, into the very earth itself. As he melted, his whole form seemed to have melted upon the face of the earth. This great rain began to come down. Liquid drops of light began to flood the very earth itself. As I watched this giant that seemed to melt, suddenly it became millions of people over the face of the earth. As I beheld the sight before me, people stood up all over the world. They were lifting their hands and they were praising the Lord.

At that very moment, there came a great thunder that seemed to roar from the heavens. I turned my eyes toward the heavens, and suddenly, I saw a figure in white, in glistening but somehow, I knew that it was the Lord Jesus Christ. He stretched forth His hand. As He did, He would stretch it forth to one, and to another, and to another; as He stretched forth His hand upon the peoples and the nations of the world – men and women. As He pointed toward them, this liquid light seemed to flow from His hand into this person and a mighty anointing of God came upon them. Those people began to go forth in the name of the Lord. I do not know how long I watched it. It seemed it went into days and weeks and months. I beheld this Christ as He continued to stretch forth His hand. But there was a tragedy. There were many people, as He stretched forth His hands that refused the anointing of God and call of God. I saw men and women that I knew, people that I felt that certainly they would receive the call of God. As He stretched forth His hand toward this one, and towards that one, they simply bowed their heads and began to back away. To each of those that seemed to bow down and back away, they seemed to go into darkness. Blackness seemed to swallow them everywhere.

I was bewildered as I watched it. These people that He had anointed covered the earth. There were hundreds of thousands of these people all over the world – in Africa, Asia, Russia, China, America – all over the world. The anointing of God was upon these people, as they went forth in the name of the Lord. I saw these men and women as they went forth. They were ditch diggers, they were washer women, they were rich men, they were poor men. I saw people who were bound with paralysis and sickness, and blindness and deafness. As the Lord stretched forth His hand to give them this anointing, they became well, they became healed – and they went forth.

This is the miracle of it. This is the glorious miracle of it. Those people would stretch forth their hands exactly as the Lord did, and it seemed that there was this same liquid fire that seemed to be in their hands. As they stretched forth their hands, they said, "According to My Word, be thou made whole." As these people continued in this mighty end–time ministry, I did not fully realize what it was. I looked to the Lord and said, "What is the meaning of this?" He said, "This is what I will do in the last days. I will restore all the cankerworm, the palmerworm, the caterpillar – I will restore all that they have destroyed. This, My people in the end–times, shall go forth and as a mighty army shall they sweep over the face of the earth."

As I was at this great height, I could behold the whole world. I watched these people as they were going to and fro over the face of the earth. Suddenly there was a man in Africa, and in a moment, he was transported by the Spirit of God, and perhaps he was in Russia, or China, or America, or some other place, and vice versa. All over the world these people came and went. They came through fire and through pestilence and through famine. Neither fire nor persecution – nothing seemed to stop them.

Angry mobs came to them with swords and with guns, and like Jesus, they passed through the multitude and they could not find them. But they went forth in the Name of the Lord. Everywhere they stretched forth their hands, the sick were healed, the blind eyes were opened. There was not a long prayer. I never saw a church, and I never saw or heard a denomination. These people were going in the name of the Lord of Hosts. As they marched forward as the ministry of Christ in the end–times: these people ministered to the multitudes over the face of the earth. Tens of thousands, even millions seemed to come to the Lord Jesus Christ, as these people went forth and gave the message of the kingdom – of the coming kingdom – in this last hour. It was so glorious! It seemed there were those that rebelled. They would become angry. They tried to attack those workers that were giving the message.

God is going to give to the world a demonstration in this last hour, such as the world has never known. These men and women will be of all walks of life. Degrees will mean nothing. I saw these workers as they were going over the face of the earth. When one would seem to stumble and fall, another would come and pick him up. There were no big "I" or little "you". Every mountain was brought low and every valley was exalted, and they seemed to have one thing in common – there was a divine love that seemed to flow forth from these people, as they walked together, and as they worked together, and lived together. It was the theme of their life. They continued and it seemed the days went by slowly, as I stood and beheld this sight. I could only cry – and sometimes I laughed. It was so wonderful as these people went throughout the face of the whole earth bringing forth God's power in this last end–times.

As I watched from the very heavens, themselves; there were times when great deluges of this liquid light seemed to fall upon great congregations. The congregations would lift their hands and seemingly praise God for hours and even days, as the Spirit of God came upon them. God said, "I will pour out My Spirit upon all flesh." And that is exactly the thing that God was doing. In fact, every man and woman that received this power and the anointing of God, had miracles of God that flowed continuously.

Suddenly there was another great clap of thunder that seemed to resound around the world. Again, I heard the voice saying: "Now, this is My people; this is My beloved bride." When the voice spoke, I looked upon the earth and I could see the lakes and the mountains. The graves were opened and people from all over the world, the saints of all ages, seemed to be rising. as they rose from the graves – suddenly all these people came from every direction – from the east and the west, from the north and the south, and they seemed to be forming again this gigantic body. As the dead in Christ seemed to be rising first, I could hardly comprehend it. It was so marvelous. It was so far beyond anything I could ever dream or even think of.

This huge body suddenly began to form and take shape again, and its' shape was in the form of the mighty giant, but this time it was different. It was arrayed in the most beautiful, gorgeous white garments. Its' garments were without spot or wrinkle as this body began to form, and the people of all ages seemed to be gathering into this body. Slowly, from the heavens above, the Lord Jesus came and became the head. I heard another clap of thunder that said, "This is My beloved bride for whom I have waited. She will come forth, even tried by fire. This is she that I have loved from the beginning of time."

As I watched, my eyes turned to the far north and I saw great destruction, men and women in anguish and crying out, and buildings destroyed. Then I heard again, the fourth voice that said, "Now is My wrath being poured out upon the face of the earth." From the ends of the whole world, it seemed that there were great vials of God's wrath being poured out upon the face of the earth. I can remember it as I beheld the awful sight of seeing the cities, and whole nations going down into destruction. I could hear the weeping and the wailing. I could hear people crying. They seemed to cry as they went into caves, and the caves and the mountains opened up. They leaped into water, but the water would not drown them. There was nothing that seemingly could destroy them. They were wanting to take their lives; but they did not succeed.

Again, I turned my eyes toward the glorious sight of this body arrayed in the beautiful white shining garments, and slowly, slowly, it began to lift from the earth, and as it did, I awoke. This sight that I had beheld was the end times ministry, in the last hour. Again, on July 27,[th] at 2:30 in the morning, the same revelation, the exact, same vision, came a second time, as it did before. My life has been changed, as I realized that we are living in the end-times, for all over the world God is anointing men and women with this ministry. It will not be doctrine. It will not be "churchianity;" but it is going to be Jesus Christ. They will give forth the Word of the Lord and are going to say – I heard it so many times in the vision – "According to My Word, it shall be done." Oh people, listen to

Me! "According to My Word, it shall be done." We are going to be clothed with power and anointing from God. We won't have to preach sermons. We won't have to preach sermons. We won't have to depend on man, nor will we be denominational echoes: but we will have the power of the living God! We will fear no man; but will go in the name of the Lord of Hosts!

Tommy Hicks died in Los Angeles, California around 1973.

# Chapter 1

## God's Seasons

In looking at the biblical principles that enforce the need for us to align ourselves in regards to our body, soul and spirit, let us examine what God's Word says about why this is an absolute prerequisite for staying well and truly free from sickness, heartache and demonic oppression. (Ecclesiastes Chapter 3: verses 1-8) say: "There is a time for everything, and a season for every purpose under the heavens:"

2  a time to be born and a time to die,
   a time to plant and a time to uproot,
3  a time to kill and a time to heal,
   a time to tear down and a time to build,
4  a time to weep and a time to laugh,
   a time to mourn and a time to dance,
5  a time to scatter stones and a time to gather them,
   a time to embrace and a time to refrain from embracing,
6  a time to search and a time to give up,
   a time to keep and a time to throw away,
7  a time to tear and a time to mend,
   a time to be silent and a time to speak,
8  a time to love and a time to hate,
   a time for war and a time for peace.

Now I want you to look particularly close at the 1st verse which says: <u>There is a time for everything, and a season for every purpose under the heavens</u>: so, what is God trying to say through this powerful verse? He is saying that yes, since we are walking through this earth in our lifetime; we will encounter challenges, strongholds, sickness and demonic oppression; but that these things are only ordained to be allowed to last <u>for a season</u>; and He further goes on to say in verse 3, there is "a time to kill and a time to heal, and time to tear down and a time to build up;' which is clearly His acknowledgement that we can destroy Satan's attacks and heal ourselves and others and we certainly can tear down every stronghold of Satan and build ourselves up both in the natural and the spiritual sense, so that we don't fall victim to Satan's devices in the same way again.

Remember also, that in (Ephesians 6:12), it says: 'For our struggle is not against flesh and blood, but against the rulers, against the authorities, against the powers of this dark world and against the spiritual forces of evil in the heavenly realms.' Well, let me tell you, that you can be a spiritual giant in God and still have sickness attack your body, through Satan's most favourite cohort, the Spirit of Infirmity. But generally, it is short term, for that same spiritual giant should presumably know what to do to make that season as short as possible. And yet, having been in some capacity of ministry myself in the last 35 years as a Pastor, Prophet or Evangelist, I have seen long term sickness literally thwart great men and women of God due to lack of knowledge, in the area of healing and spiritual warfare. As a spirit filled Christian myself, I am convinced that Satan cannot touch our Spirits with his targeted attacks, if our feet are firmly on the rock of Jesus and we are following Him with our whole hearts.

However, I have seen time and time again, in my ministry of healing and prophecy, prayer. that Satan looks for open doors, so that he can attack us through our souls (which encompasses our mind and emotions); and through our bodies, which oftentimes we neglect with poor eating habits, lack of exercise, and by having very little peace and relaxation in our lives.

Distractions and an overburdening of a Christian is a tried and tested method that Satan uses to attack our minds and bodies; because as we get our eyes on the problems, then harassment comes and sometimes this sort of demonic oppression can seem unending. Through this method, Satan is able to neutralise a Christian to such an extreme level, that he or she is in a kind of spiritual shock. Now other than a minister, I also am a trained nurse and the definition of shock is as follows: 'A jarring surprise, like the shock of getting fired, or when the human body goes into a state of shock, he or she is at a state of near collapse, reeling from a traumatic situation or event.' Within the human body, if there is severe physical trauma, then the body uses shock as a defence mechanism to block out painful memories or pain. In the case of spiritual shock, we tend to block out both good and bad influences; and just go into "survival mode," which is exactly what the enemy wants. Because, if we are not reaching out to God and taking steps to improve our situation, then the season whether it be illness or demonic oppression, can last for a very long time, without any victory whatsoever."

So how can we truly resist Satan, so that He will flee from our lives, as is stated In God's Word, in James 4:7: 'Submit yourselves, then, to God. Resist the devil, and he will flee from you.' Well beloved, we can absolutely resist Satan; but we must have an in depth understanding of "submitting ourselves to God' and what this truly entails to ensure victory is achieved in every area of our lives as Christians. Commitment, focus, and being able to hear God's instructions for our lives and growing in spiritual wisdom, so that we have applicable battle plans to defeat the enemy at every turn, is a good start. For God has already provided ample weaponry and provisions to ensure our victory against Satan; but with very little knowledge of how to use the weaponry or implement the provisions; we often times are like children going into battle and are easy targets for Satan to overcome each and every day.

And so, let us go back to the discussion about God ordaining seasons for all things, and let us examine the question. Does He at times, allow sickness to linger a bit longer in a person's life to accomplish a purpose, even though they are doing everything possible to cause the infirmity to go? Well, I can confirm that this has happened in my own life, when I have not taken care of my body properly and He is trying to teach me a better way to do this; and also, I can remember one experience, that I had, when I came down with pneumonia and was in the hospital for 11 days and during that time God enabled me to meet a very discouraged, spirit filled, Polish doctor, who needed my prayers and encouragement very badly. I believe God used my husband and I during that time, to encourage that young doctor by telling of my healing ministry in which God worked mighty miracles in many people's lives; and we also prayed together several times.

By the last day, I can report that he left rejoicing in the Lord Jesus, encouraged and fired up to go and do the work of the Lord. An additional blessing was that I was feeling much better by the $9^{th}$ day and was healed completely by the Lord, once my stay in the hospital was over, Praise God!

# Chapter 2

## The Truth About Negative Open Doors

There is a lot of condemnation directed towards Christians these days, in that some people believe that if a person is sick or injured; then it is entirely caused by the fact that the person is in sin. But the truth is, open doors to demon oppression can happen due to a number of reasons, and many of them occur; because of a lack of understanding. Although, I will admit that direct, wilful sin can certainly be one of them. Demonic oppression can certainly occur because of the following reasons:

1. Direct Wilful Sin
2. The Occult
3. Inheritance – Generational
4. Unforgiveness
5. Trauma
6. Abuse/Immorality
7. Ungodly Soul Ties
8. Witchcraft Curses
9. Addictions
10. Fears and Phobias
11. False Religions
12. Cursed Objects

## 13. Cursed Buildings

This a fairly exhaustive list; and certainly, worth considering if you fall into any of these categories. Generational curses can occur if a sinful generation has not repented and continues to engage in the sin. For most assuredly, either they or the next generation need to repent before God and turn away from that sin altogether. This is important because even if the next generation has not engaged in the sin, the door has already been opened by the former generation; and demonic oppression has firmly established itself within that family.

Equally, generational blessings can abound, if the former generation has walked obediently in God's statutes and lived victoriously in their Christian walk. For without a doubt, future generations will be mightily blessed, if this is the case, as long as, they too walk in obedience to God. (Deuteronomy 11:26-28) says "See, I am setting before you today a blessing and a curse, the blessing if you obey the commands of the LORD your God that I am giving you today; the curse if you disobey the commands of the LORD your God, and turn from the way that I command you today by following other gods, which you have not known.

Beloved, I am in agreement that it is not fair that seemingly innocent people must put up with demonic oppression, if it was foisted upon them by violence or generational curses, or poor habits; but truthfully, Satan does not play fair and he will seek whatever means possible to destroy God's People. 1 Peter 5:8 says "Be alert and of sober mind. Your enemy the devil prowls around like a roaring lion looking for someone to devour"

During my years of pastoral counselling, I came to the conclusion, that most sexually perverse lifestyles occur from sexual immorality being introduced in some explicit form whilst the person has been in childhood. This is very sad, but also very shrewd of Satan, for once he can take over a person's life in such a way, he then has a powerful hold over that person's mind, emotions and body, which can cause immense fallout in a person's life and cause destructive ramifications for many generations to come.

Soul ties can be positive and can be negative.

In a Godly marriage, God links the two people together and the Bible tells us that they become one flesh. And as a result of them becoming one flesh, it binds them together and they will cleave onto one another in a unique way. The purpose of this cleaving is to build a very healthy, strong and close relationship between a man and a woman.

*(Matthew 19:5) says, "And said, for this reason <u>shall a man leave father and mother and shall cleave to his wife: and they twain shall be one flesh</u>."*

Soul ties can also be found in close friendships. They are not just limited to marriage, as we can see with King David and Jonathan:

*(1 Samuel 18:1), "And it came to pass, when he had made an end of speaking unto Saul, that <u>the soul of Jonathan was knit with the soul of David</u>, and Jonathan loved him as his own soul."*

The negative effect of a soul tie is when a soul tie can be used for the devil's advantage. Such as, soul ties formed from sex outside of marriage, causing a person to become defiled:

This is spoken about in: *(Genesis 34:2-3), "And when Shechem the son of Hamor, the Hivite, prince of the country, saw her, he took her, and <u>lay with her, and defiled her. And his soul cleaved unto Dinah,</u> the daughter of Jacob, and he loved the damsel, and spoke kindly unto the damsel."*

This is why, it is so common for a person to still have 'feelings' towards an ex-lover, that they have no right to be attracted to in that way. Even 20 years later, a person may still think of their first lover... even if he or she is across the country and has their own family, all because of a soul tie! As a result, demonic spirits can take advantage of ungodly soul ties, and use them to transfer spirits between one person to another. Such people can face severe demonic visitations and torment, all thanks to an ungodly soul tie. However, the good news is, that once the soul tie is broken and repented of, the attacks, if resisted, will stop completely.

Let us now talk about how important it is, not to be vehicles of condemnation or fault finding towards others. I have noticed in my own life and in others I have known, that when we achieve a higher level of victory, as we seek after our full alignment with God; that Satan often tries to oppress God's people with a Spirit of Pride; which causes great destruction in that person's own life, and also, to those they are speaking against. And quite simply this sort of behaviour can be catastrophic. With this in mind, we must safeguard ourselves, so that we do not fall victim to this ploy of the enemy. You see beloved, many people in the Body of Christ tend to take on the attitude that "if I was able to shorten that season of trials by applying God's principles, then why can't Sally or Rob do the same?' and consequently, this prideful and critical attitude opens a door for Satan to firmly take hold of us with this destructive spirit. Remember, what the Word says in (Proverbs 16:18), 'That Pride goes before destruction and a haughty spirit before a fall. Furthermore, just like in the army in the natural, there may be Generals (Pastors, Evangelists, or Prophetic Leaders) or Privates (lay people); but each one needs the other in order to make an effective army and this is just the same in the Body of Christ. Because God loves us all equally and has an important part for each of us to play in His end time harvest.

Just to underscore this point, God speaks about this in his Word in (Isaiah, Chapter 11:1-9): 'And there shall come forth a rod out of the stem of Jesse, and a Branch shall grow out of his roots: And the Spirit of the LORD shall rest upon him, the spirit of wisdom and understanding, the spirit of counsel and might, the spirit of knowledge and of the fear of the LORD; And shall make him of quick understanding in the fear of the LORD: and he shall not judge after the sight of his eyes, neither reprove after the hearing of his ears: But with righteousness shall he judge the poor, and reprove with equity for the meek of the earth: and he shall smite the earth with the rod of his mouth, and with the breath of his lips shall he slay the wicked. And righteousness shall be the girdle of his loins, and faithfulness the girdle of his reins. The wolf also shall dwell with the lamb, and the leopard shall lie down with the kid; and the calf and the young lion and the fatling together; and a little child shall lead them...They shall not hurt nor destroy in all my holy mountain: for the earth shall be full of the knowledge of the LORD, as the waters cover the sea. Beloved, we are the very identity of Jesus Christ, as His children, and we should personify Him in everything we do.

So, we must seek wholeheartedly to align ourselves in humility, wisdom and grace and not allow our differences nor even the slow progression of our brothers and sisters towards a place of victory deter us. For Jesus walked on this earth in patience, humility, love and compassion; and if we do the same, then this will ensure that victory reigns supreme in our lives and the lives of others surrounding us, of whom we seek to help.

You might say 'But Leisa, this is too hard, because I am just a human being and not a superhero.' But let me encourage you, that God will guide you and protect you in your journey towards being aligned in body, soul, and spirit with His purposes, every step of the way. The Lord promises us this in the dearly beloved scripture verse, (Psalm 23:4): 'Yea, though I walk through the valley of the shadow of death, I will fear no evil: for Thou *art* with me; Thy rod and Thy staff they comfort me.' Remember Beloved, that the 'valley of the shadow of death' is just a season you are passing through; and that both 'His rod and His staff shall comfort us.' A shepherd often uses his rod to defend his sheep and his staff is used to guide them; and so, it is with God. He will guide us as we walk through sickness, emotional upheaval, and demonic oppression; until we get to a place of total victory. So, now that we know what we are facing and the reasons for it, in the following chapters let us look at what we can do to thwart the enemy, so that we can move into a greater place of blessing and joy, as God leads us to our ordained destiny in Him. Hallelujah!

# Chapter 3

## The Defilement of Food
## Through the Spirit of Mammon

There are plenty of books out there these days encouraging people to eat healthy. But I think it is important to understand in the Body of Christ, what is happening in the market place which impacts not only food being sold in grocery stores and restaurants; but also determines how being blind to the plans and schemes of the enemy in this area; can actually have devastating effects upon God's people. For not only obesity, but actual disease conditions can be the direct result of these toxic practices which can severely hinder and shorten our lives.

There is a definite agenda amongst food manufacturers and distributors around the world, to ensure they make as much money as possible. This entails making their foods last as long as possible by putting large amounts of preservatives in their food products being sold, which enables them to sell food in a variety of ways, such as frozen foods in grocery stores and restaurants In addition, these food manufacturing giants are mixing their foods with high concentrations of sugar and salt, and chemicals of every description, to ensure they induce people to keep buying their products again and again, purely based on flavour. And these food giants are motivated by a worldwide principality called the "Spirit of Mammon."

The word "mammon" is mentioned in the Bible four times and three of those times Jesus spoke about the word. But what does it mean? Mammon is an Aramaic word that essentially means "riches." And at its' very core, this demonic entity promotes the agenda that man does not need God and that he or she can be self-sufficient and just trust in riches. In (Matthew 6:24), Jesus clearly suggests it is possible to serve mammon instead of serving God; and He goes further and says, "It is impossible to serve both at the same time." He further says, 'you will love one and hate the other,' and emphasises that there is no middle ground. Did you know that all money has a spirit on it? It is either the Spirit of God to do tremendous good or the Spirit of Mammon by default; and Satan then uses it for his purposes. That is why people think money can bring them happiness and fulfilment. Let's be honest, mammon is basically the spirit of the world and that is never good news for God's people.

Recently, I read an account of a man who had stored an old coat in his attic and basically had forgotten all about it. But then 15 years later, he decided that he wanted to donate some clothes to charity and whilst rummaging through his clothes in the attic found in the right-hand pocket of his old coat, a fully wrapped fast food hamburger. I mean, one might expect the food product to be full of mould and to have a horrible smell; but in fact, the hamburger was perfectly preserved, as if the man had only bought it the day before. This demonstrates the strength and magnitude of the preservative used in that hamburger, and the truth is, many studies through the years, have determined that the human body does not even recognise a preservative when it goes through the digestive system. As a result, it is either stored as fat or designated to some other sinister purpose within the human body.

The positive spin that food manufacturers give to validate their reasons for using preservatives, is that they prevent bacteria growth and spoilage. And while the effects of food preservatives on the body can vary with age and health status, looking into the potential harmful effects of preservatives in foods will help you reclaim good health and protect your personal well-being against toxic damage. So, let us look at what scientists say can be the potential devastating effects of such toxins.

**Breathing Difficulties:**

One of the harmful effects of preservatives in foods is the potential to cause breathing difficulties. According to MayoClinic.com, eliminating foods with preservatives from the diet can reduce the symptoms and severity of asthma. MayoClinic.com identified aspartame, sulphites, benzoates and yellow dye No. 5, as preservatives that could exacerbate breathing problems in asthmatics and others, while Medical News Today linked sulphites with shortness of breath and other breathing problems.

**Behavioural Changes:**

Another harmful effect of preservatives in foods is behavioural changes, especially in young children. According to the Archives of Disease in Children, in a 2003 double-blind study of 1,873 children, the consumption of food additives and preservatives led to a significant increase in hyperactive behaviour. Removing the preservatives or using a placebo didn't lead to these behaviours, which were measured by both parental and objective reporting.

**Heart Damage:**
Studies of heart tissue reviewed by InChem have shown that food preservatives can weaken heart tissues. According to laboratory research, rats who consumed the highest levels of food preservatives showed the highest levels of heart damage over time.

**Cancer:**
One of the most serious harmful effects of preservatives in foods is their ability to transform into carcinogens when digested. According to InChem, nitrosamines, which include nitrites and nitrates, interact with stomach and gastric acids to form cancer-causing agents. To avoid this natural chemical reaction between your body and the preservatives, you will need to monitor your diet to eliminate nitrates and nitrites from your meals, snacks and beverages.

So, what can we do to cut down the amount of preservatives in our diets and not expose ourselves to these terrible health risks? Well, eliminate frozen foods and fast food restaurant foods from our diets for a start, and I would also recommend reading food labels and becoming educated to what foods contain the worst and heaviest amounts of preservatives out there in the marketplace. Frankly, if you cannot pronounce an ingredient on a label, it is probably best not to eat it. Believe me, there are many dangerous food additives and preservatives in foods being sold today, that we all need to be aware of, and avoid. Let's have a look at some of the worst ones to avoid below:

- **Butylated Hydroxyanisole:** This preservative is mainly found in foods that have a high fat content such as meats, butters, snack foods and even beer. Test results on this preservative have been inconclusive thus far, but have shown that high doses do promote tumour cell growth in animals.

- **Sodium Nitrate:** How this is viewed as safe is beyond me, because the U.S. Environmental Protection Agency says: 'that high levels of exposure are linked to increased cancer rate and may be related to brain tumours, leukaemia and nose and throat tumours in children.' Sodium Nitrate is common in packaged deli meats and smoked meat, such as bacon and jerky.

- **Ammonium Sulfate:** Ammonium is often used as a cleaning product and the labels have warnings on ingestion, but this product is often used to make many breads! In fact, large amounts of consumptions can lead to irritation of the gastrointestinal tract, nausea, vomiting and diarrhoea. So, be sure to look at the ingredients when you buy your next loaf of bread!

- **Monosodium Glutamate (MSG):** MSG is an amino acid often found in Asian foods, potato chips, salad dressing and frozen entrees. It is linked to causing headaches and nausea.

- **Potassium Bromate:** This ingredient is a little more rare; but is one of the most dangerous out there. So, be sure to check the label for this one. In fact, in California, bread makers that use Potassium Bromate are required to put a cancer label on their products!

- **Aspartame:** Is known as the most dangerous substance added to foods. There are many side effects that are linked to consuming large amounts of Aspartame including: migraines, nausea, muscle spasms, insomnia, heart palpitations, diabetes and even memory loss. This product is often found in common sodas and dried goods. They even put this in many "diet" foods, so be sure to check the ingredient labels when you think you are purchasing a healthy product.

- **High Fructose Corn Syrup:** Is the most common artificial sweetener. It is found in many sodas and flavoured drinks, but it is also found in many condiments in the fast food industry. High Fructose Corn Syrup is linked to obesity and can induce terrible cravings for sweet foods, which can result with possible diabetic issues.

- **Olestra:** is found mainly in baked and fried foods. Olestra is linked to gastrointestinal disease, diarrhoea, gas, cramps, bleeding and incontinence.

- **Brominated Vegetable Oil:** Is found mainly in citrus flavoured drinks and soda. It is known to damage the liver, testicles, thyroid, heart and kidneys.

- **Shortening/Partially Hydrogenated Oil:** This is linked to obesity and clogging of arteries, but on top of that it also increases risk of metabolic syndrome.

Beloved, it is important that you understand what God's Word says about how we are to eat; because God wants us to walk in divine health and He has provided natural and healthy foods to partake of, as is described in (Genesis 1: 29-30): ''Then God said, Behold, I have given you every plant yielding seed that is on the surface of all the earth, and every tree which has fruit yielding seed; it shall be food for you; and to every beast of the earth and to every bird of the sky and to everything that moves on the earth which has life, I have given every green plant for food"; and it was so.'

And yet, through the Spirit of Mammon, this food is being defiled as is spoken about in (Exodus 34:15): 'otherwise you might make a covenant with the inhabitants of the land and they would play the harlot with their gods and sacrifice to their gods, and someone might invite you to eat of his sacrifice,' Please understand beloved, that the Spirit of Mammon owns the market place and is inviting us to buy and eat food which has been defiled for the benefit of making money. And Mammon or riches is indeed the god of these food manufacturers, not the wellbeing of the people who are eating their products, which is the sad, but irrevocable truth of the matter in today's world.

# Chapter 4

## God's Provisioning Versus Satan's Counterfeits

God has been speaking to my heart that He is granting His people a great provisioning from the heavenlies for the latter days. However, as he makes provision for His people we must not be fooled into partaking of things, that look to be of God; but in actuality are in fact, a counterfeit which Satan has created to hinder God's people from divine health and peace of mind.

The Prophet Jeremiah lived in a time that was very difficult for the Hebrew people; because of their disobedience to God's laws. Jeremiah was the son of Hilkiah, a Jewish priest from the Benjamite village of Anathoth. Jeremiah was called to prophetic ministry c. 626 BC and was called by God to give prophecy of Jerusalem's destruction that would occur by invaders from the north. This was because Israel had been unfaithful to the laws of the covenant and had forsaken God by worshiping Baal. The people of Israel had even gone as far as building high altars to Baal, in order to burn their children in fire and offer them as sacrifices. That nation had deviated so far from God that they had broken their covenant with Him, causing God to withdraw his blessings entirely. Jeremiah was guided by God to proclaim that the nation of Judah would be faced with famine, and plundered and taken captive by foreigners, who would exile them to a foreign land. But let us look at his mandate to expose counterfeit or false prophets (which had they been listened to by the Hebrew people) would have been counterproductive to the fate and welfare of God's people for generations to come. First of all, God proclaimed His goodness towards His people after they had been taken captive, in (Jeremiah 29: 11): "For I know the plans I have for you," declares the LORD, "plans to prosper you and not to harm you, plans to give you hope and a future." And then He proclaimed in (Jeremiah 29:12-14), that although they had walked in blindness and disobedience and opened up doors to sickness, demonic oppression and ultimately loss of the homes and their way of life; that He was providing a way for them to be restored, as is written in these following verses "Then you will call on me and come and pray to me, and I will listen to you. You will seek me and find me when you seek me with all your heart. [14] I will be found by you," declared the LORD, "and will bring you back from captivity.[c] I will gather you from all the nations and places where I have banished you," declared the LORD, "and will bring you back to the place from which I carried you into exile." But all the while, Satan had raised up lying prophets or voices within the midst of these oppressed people, to speak an opposing or counterfeit truth. Jeremiah spoke staunchly against these men, as God's mouthpiece and later in Chapter 29, ultimate destruction was their fate.

Just as Jeremiah did, we must expose these counterfeits which Satan has created for the purpose of destroying God's people; and then we must walk boldly into the true provisioning that God has arranged for us through his compassion and grace. Counterfeits can be in be seen in all aspects of our daily life; but mostly in the things we choose to focus upon or partake of, and if these are not God's provisioning, then most certainly a season of trials will be our portion. (Psalm 23:5) says: *"You prepare a table before me in the presence of my enemies: you anoint my head with oil; my cup runs over."* In other words, we can eat of the Lord's Table of provision, in spite of the temptations all around us, and if we choose wisely and take our portion from the Lord's Table and nowhere else, then we will avoid health issues and demonic oppression. To give you some examples in reference to God's natural healing power, it is important that you ensure you eat the things that are good for you; and for you to turn to some natural remedies that God has provided in nature. There are an abundance of things in nature to use if you do feel unwell; and believe me beloved, if we rely on God's provisions, there will be less need for us to be victims of sickness or the spirit of infirmity.

So, what are a few examples of remedies God has provided through nature; that can be of great benefit to our overall health?

- Honey reduces inflammation markedly in the human body and most doctors when doing health checks will order a test called a C Reactive Protein Test, which will check a person's inflammatory markers. Why not include honey in your diet to keep the swelling in your body to a minimum? Honey also lowers both the LDL (bad) Cholesterol and will help to fight plague build up in a person's arteries. Remarkably, Honey also lowers the

Homocysteine level within a person's body which is the blood marker for disease.
- Cumin and Turmeric Herbs are excellent anti-inflammatory, plague fighters and help decrease swelling and a build-up of protein in the brain; which is particularly key in respect to people who have been afflicted with brain injury or brain related diseases like Alzheimer's disease.
- Pennyroyal, Hyssop, and Thyme Herbs can help breathlessness and specifically, can help asthmatic and lung disease victims.
- Fennel Herbs are extremely good for Heart health and blood pressure.

These are just a few examples of God's natural provisioning and how making wise choices like these, coupled with prayer and a positive confession of God's healing power; can work wonders in moving us towards divine healing in a very tangible way. But beware beloved of the counterfeits being sold in stores and restaurants and remember that there are man-made preservatives and chemicals hidden in flavourful foods, which means we must safeguard ourselves from Satan's cunning plan to destroy our health.

Let us talk briefly about people that suffer terribly from pollen and mold allergies. It is important to realise that God talks about mildew, which is more commonly known as mould, in (Leviticus 14:33-42), which is a prevalent cause of sinus allergies. The passage says: 'The Lord said to Moses and Aaron, when you enter the land of Canaan, which I am giving you as your possession, and I put a spreading mould in a house in that land, the owner of the house must go and tell the priest, 'I have seen something that looks like a defiling mold in my house.' The priest is to order the house to be emptied before he goes in to examine the mold, so that nothing in the house will be pronounced unclean. After this the priest is to go in and inspect the house. He is to examine the mold on the walls, and if it has greenish or reddish depressions that appear to be deeper than the surface of the wall, the priest shall go out the doorway of the house and close it up for seven days. On the seventh day the priest shall return to inspect the house. If the mold has spread on the walls, he is to order that the contaminated stones be torn out and thrown into an unclean place outside the town. He must have all the inside walls of the house scraped and the material that is scraped off dumped into an unclean place outside the town. Then they are to take other stones to replace these and take new clay and plaster the house.

The symptoms of mold or mildew exposure include sneezing, runny nose, coughing, wheezing, watery and itchy eyes, and skin rash. And it can most definitely exacerbate asthma symptoms; and most certainly removing the mold from your environment is God's preferred option. However, there are natural remedies God has provided to help allergy symptoms. Most of us are aware that pollens are caused primarily by allergies to dust, grass and trees, and is sometimes worsened due to things we eat.

A few years ago, I developed a liking for Camomile tea and I was convinced its' calming effects were helping me. But little did I know at the time, that my heightened pollen allergy sensitivity and symptoms were a direct result of drinking that tea. In reality, Camomile herbs are very similar to Ragweed and if you are sensitive to one, you will most certainly be sensitive to the other; and so, once I became aware of that fact, I stopped drinking Camomile tea. And as a result, my symptoms immediately improved. So, let us look at some natural remedies God has provided for pollen and mold allergies, which may help you with this bothersome complaint.

- Nettle leaf can be used in combination with other herbs to make a soothing herbal tea for allergy relief. It is often mixed with peppermint leaf and sometimes red raspberry leaf to make a refreshing allergy relief tea.
- Quercetin is a key flavonoid widely distributed in nature and is found in many foods which can help fight against allergy symptoms. A list of foods containing this vital ingredient is as follows:
- Apples.
- Peppers.
- Red wine.
- Dark cherries and berries (blueberries, bilberries, blackberries and others)
- Tomatoes.
- Cruciferous veggies, including broccoli, cabbage and sprouts.
- Leafy green veggies, including spinach, and kale.

# Chapter 5

## Reasons and Seasons of Sickness

As A teenager, I was an avid athlete and I would compete in various races throughout the year. But unfortunately, I found that on the day of the track meets, I would often have tremendous stomach pains and other accompanying terrible symptoms; which were directly related to the impact my emotions or mind (soul), were having upon my physical body. This is an example of the power that the soul can have over our bodies and is precisely why Satan seeks to control our souls through his various attacks and devices in this way.

In the Bible, it talks about the disciple Timothy and his stomach problems and about his "frequent infirmities" and about Paul's advice concerning those infirmities. And many people in the Christian world have wondered why God just didn't work supernaturally though Paul to heal Timothy, for after all wasn't this part of Paul's ministry "signs, wonders, and miracles?" And for that matter, why did Paul have sickness, for he also spoke about "a thorn" of sickness in his own life?

Beloved, God often allows sickness for a season in our lives for His purposes; and usually it is either to teach and emphasize something in our lives, or to bring about salvation in others or indeed both. In Timothy's case: Paul advised in (1 Timothy 5:23) to: "No longer drink only water; but use a little wine for his stomach's sake and his frequent infirmities."

When you read this passage, you see very clearly that Paul is telling Timothy how to "avoid" getting sick so often; and also, is giving advice as to how Timothy can relieve his symptoms." The truth is, Paul was in fact, trying to advise his young disciple on a very practical level. You see, in those days and times, the water supply would often be contaminated, and Paul was trying to open Timothy's eyes, as to what this contaminated water was doing to his body. Paul wasn't getting all "spooky spiritual" about his advice, he was merely pointing out the natural open door which had allowed the Spirit of Infirmity to take hold of Timothy's body, and was causing him to be oppressed in both his body and his mind. And by recommending that wine be added to the water, Paul was meaning that its' antiseptic qualities would have a purifying effect on the water and would enable it to cause less sickness.

In the case of allowing sickness for a season for the purpose of salvation, I can wholeheartedly confirm that this does happen. Recently in fact, in my own Dad's life, at the age of 79, he was savagely struck down with a large blood clot in the back of his brain. And at the time, the surgeons had only given him a few days to live. Suddenly, my dad was in an intensive care unit and was hooked up to a ventilator and various machines and was semi-comatosed. So, I flew 10,000 miles to be with him, and was shocked to see my Dad brought to such a terrible place, as he had always been a very robust and healthy man. He had accepted the Lord as his personal saviour when I was 14 years old, but since then, he had rejected God due to a series of events which had happened in his life; and so I started praying the minute I walked into his hospital room for his salvation, because I did not want my Dad going to Hell! My brother joined me later on in my Dad's hospital room, and said 'He had experienced a dream the night before and in the dream that he and our dad were standing in a place and that our dad was slipping into the very depths of Hell; and that he (my brother) had been pulling him out with all of his might.' My brother then told me, 'that he had awoken from the dream and had looked in the mirror and there had been a bruise on the front of his chest, where he had been pressing against a surface for leverage, in order to pull our dad out of the pits of Hell.' He then showed me the bruise and we began praying night and day for our dad's salvation. The surgeons came in two days later and said 'there was no hope and urged us to turn off all of our dad's machines; and just to let him go peacefully'; but I was not about to give up that easily. "For I remembered what the word says in (Matthew 11:12): "And from the days of John the Baptist until now, the kingdom of Heaven suffers violence and the violent take it by force." For just as so many men and women in the Bible, earnestly prayed to God to turn their situations around for good; so, I likewise prayed night and day for the salvation of our dad.

Miraculously, five days later our dad was still alive and getting better and he was alert and trying to speak and I urged the doctors to order a cat scan to be conducted to check his progress. Gloriously, the blood clot in the back of our dad's brain was so shrivelled up, that the doctors' declared that there had been a "modern day miracle." Hallelujah! Beloved, my dad did die three months later due to pneumonia; but only after gloriously recommitting his life back to the Lord Jesus Christ. And I am so very grateful for the extra time that God gave our dad to get his life right with Him, even though he had to endure such a devastating season of sickness to get to that place.

Many ailments are quite commonplace amongst human beings and such afflictions can bring about great distress both physically and mentally within a person. And so, we must look for ways in which we may not only alleviate the symptoms; but so that we can prevent this type of illness coming upon us altogether. The methods of eating correctly and being aware of open doors which may cause anxiety and stress in our lives are the first steps towards healing in our bodies. To end these afflictions and to close the open doors of these complaints should be the main goal; as we open up a new door of long standing, divine health. We can then proclaim the powerful scripture verse in (Revelations 3:8); "'I know your deeds. Behold, I have put before you an open door which no one can shut, because you have a little power, and have kept My word, and have not denied My name."

In regard to modern day stomach ailments, after working many years as a nurse, I have found that most of these symptoms are caused by either food intolerance or food allergies. Food intolerance is a digestive system response rather than an immune system response. It occurs when something in food irritates a person's digestive system or when a person is unable to properly digest, or break down, their food. Intolerance to lactose, which is found in milk and other dairy products, is the most common food intolerance.

A food allergy is an immune system response, and is caused when the body mistakes an ingredient in food, usually a protein, as harmful and creates a defense system (antibodies) to fight it. An allergic reaction occurs when the antibodies are battling an "invading" food protein. The most common food allergies are shellfish, nuts, fish, eggs, peanuts and milk.

The symptoms of food intolerance are:
- Nausea
- Stomach pain
- Gas, cramps or bloating
- Vomiting
- Heartburn
- Diarrhoea
- Headaches
- Irritability or nervousness

The symptoms of food allergies are:
- Nausea
- Rash or hives
- Cramping stomach pain
- Diarrhoea
- Itchy skin
- Shortness of breath
- Chest pain
- Swelling of the airways to the lungs

Please note food allergies can be life threatening and must be taken seriously.

**How common are food allergies and intolerances?**

Food allergies affect about 1 percent of adults and 7 percent of children, although, some children outgrow their allergies.

Food intolerances are much more common. In fact, nearly everyone at one time has had an unpleasant reaction to something they ate. Some people have specific food intolerances. Lactose intolerance is the most common specific food intolerance and affects about 10 percent of western populations.

**So, what causes food allergies and intolerances?**

Well, medical experts say, 'that food allergies arise from sensitivity to chemical compounds (proteins) in food, and even to some compounds that are found naturally in food.' In addition, they say that 'food allergies are more common in people whose family members have allergies, suggesting a genetic or hereditary factor may be involved with the development of food allergies.' And so, from a spiritual perspective we must be aware of the schemes of the enemy through not only the foods that we are challenged with, but also through generational curses which have been passed down to us, due to sin or indeed open doors which have been left ajar, by those in our family that have lived before us. If there is sin involved, then of course we can repent on behalf of our forefathers to close the door; but then we must also bring our bodies into alignment and address the physical ravages that such sin conditions have caused and develop a new way of living to ensure the healing of our bodies is achieved in the long term.

From a purely scientific perspective, food allergies develop after we are exposed to a food protein that our body thinks is harmful. As a result, the first time we eat the food containing the protein, our immune systems respond by creating specific disease-fighting antibodies (called immunoglobulin E or IgE). And when we eat the food again, it triggers the release of IgE antibodies and other chemicals, including histamine, in an effort to expel the protein "invader" from our bodies. Histamine is a powerful chemical that can affect the respiratory system, gastrointestinal tract, skin or cardiovascular system.

The allergy symptoms we have depends entirely upon where in the body the histamine is released. If it is released in the ears, nose and throat, we may have an itchy nose and mouth, or trouble breathing or swallowing. If the histamine is released in the skin, we may develop hives or a rash. And if the histamine is released in the gastrointestinal tract, we likely will develop stomach pains, cramps or diarrhoea. Many people experience a combination of symptoms, as the food is eaten and digested. Beloved, the instance of food allergies within human beings has increased greatly since the introduction of preservatives and chemicals into our diets and this cannot be denied.

In fact, most meats being sold today have preservative ingredients in them called sodium nitrate and nitrites. These ingredients help to prevent oxidation of meats, keeping them red in colour and preventing bacterial growth. The U.S. Environmental Protection Agency notes that consumption of nitrates may be linked to an increased risk of cancers, such as leukaemia, brain tumours and nasopharyngeal tumours. Nitrates and nitrites may also increase risk for diabetes, diarrhoea and respiratory tract infections in children. And ingesting a large amount of these preservatives at one time may cause you to experience abdominal pain, muscle weakness, bloody stools and fainting, according to the EPA. You'll find nitrates and nitrites in bacon, lunch meat, hot dogs, sausage, smoked fish, ham and corned beef.

Preservative ingredients called Sulfites in dried fruit, wine, shrimp and processed potato foods help prevent discoloration in food. They also destroy vitamin B-1 content. If you are sensitive to Sulfites, you may experience skin irritations, hives, flushing, hypotension, abdominal pain, diarrhoea and asthmatic breathing after eating them, according to a study published in November 2009 in the journal "Clinical and Experimental Allergy." The U.S. Food and Drug Administration continues to allow the use of Sulfites in food, and strangely the preservative appears on the "Generally Recognized as Safe" list.

Sodium benzoate, or benzoic acid, is another preservative used to prevent bacterial growth in foods. The Centre for Science in the Public Interest notes 'that people who are sensitive to sodium benzoate may experience hives, asthma or allergic reactions after consuming it.' When combined with vitamin C, also known as ascorbic acid, sodium benzoate may pose a small risk of cancer, including leukaemia. According to the World Health Organization, animal studies reveal that high doses of the preservative may cause damage to the heart, spleen, liver, kidneys, brain and adrenal glands. But human studies and studies with lower consumption rates are limited.

There are many factors that may contribute to food intolerance. In some cases — as with lactose intolerance — the person lacks the chemicals, called enzymes, necessary to properly digest certain proteins found in food. Also, very common, are intolerances to some chemical ingredients added to food to provide color, enhance taste and protect against the growth of bacteria. These ingredients include various dyes and monosodium glutamate (MSG), a flavour enhancer.

So how can you tell the difference between an allergy and intolerance to food?

Food allergies can be triggered by even a small amount of the food and occur every time the food is consumed. People with food allergies are generally advised to avoid the offending foods completely. On the other hand, food intolerances often are dose related; people with food intolerance may not have symptoms unless they eat a large portion of the food or eat the food frequently. For example, a person with lactose intolerance may be able to drink milk in coffee or a single glass of milk but becomes sick if he or she drinks several glasses of milk. Food allergies and intolerances also are different from food poisoning, which generally results from spoiled or tainted food and affects more than one person eating the food.

So how can we eliminate such upset and risk to our digestion and indeed our bodies?

**Add probiotics to your life:**

Probiotics are strains of beneficial bacteria that live in your digestive system. These bacteria are microorganisms called "probiotics" which means 'for life'. These microscopic 'bugs' live in your intestines where they produce vitamins and short-chain fatty acids that feed and nurture other beneficial bacteria, which are non-pathogenic (non-disease causing) and directly contribute to a healthy gut flora (the community of bacteria in your gut). These bacteria aid in digestion (breaking down the foods you eat), help prevent infection and reduce chronic inflammation. These can be added to our diets by eating raw fermented foods like kefir, yogurt, sauerkraut, kimchi and kombucha.

**Change your eating habits:**
The way you eat has a large impact on how your digestive system works. By changing a few of your eating habits you may be able to improve your digestion dramatically. These are a few of my favourite good digestion behaviour tips:

First, eat in a relaxed environment and focus on eating. Turn off the television and phone so you can fully focus on the food you are eating and the act of eating. Notice how your food looks, tastes, smells and feels in your mouth. This is called being mindful and try not to eat when you are upset or in a bad mood. Your brain and your digestive tract are interconnected, so these feelings can impact the effectiveness of your digestive system, believe me.

Also, be sure to chew each mouthful of food thoroughly before swallowing it to lessen the impact on your digestive system. Chewing your food into smaller particles is an essential, but often overlooked, step in digestion. The more you chew your food, the better it will be broken down which will help with the digestive process. This is because breaking down your food mechanically is actually considered to be the first phase of digestion. The smaller the particles, the easier the food travels down the oesophagus. Because, as you chew your food, saliva is released from glands in your mouth and this begins the chemical digestion of the food before it even reaches your stomach. Additionally, the presence of saliva triggers the stomach to produce acid and its' own digestive enzymes in preparation for the arrival of your meal. The act of chewing is often the most overlooked step in the digestive process; but not one to be taken lightly. Sounds too simple, right? Beloved, we must realise that God created our digestive systems to work perfectly, it is only our poor habits coupled with defiled or preservative polluted food that causes us such distress in our gut, so let us change our eating patterns and daily habits, so that we may work with God's perfected design not against it. (Romans 12: 1-2) says: Therefore, I urge you, brothers and sisters, in view of God's mercy, to offer your bodies as a living sacrifice, holy and pleasing to God—this is your true and proper worship. Do not conform to the pattern of this world, but be transformed by the renewing of your mind. Then you will be able to test and approve what God's will is—His good, pleasing and perfect will.

**Stay hydrated:**

Water is important for digestion! We need water to digest solid food and absorb nutrients properly. Without water, the entire body's performance decreases which can lead to dehydration and decrease blood pressure which can cause constipation. Drink enough water each day. The average person should aim to consume approximately 80 ounces of water (or other non-caffeinated fluids) each day. But…you need to drink this water between meals rather than with meals to avoid diluting stomach acid which is vital for *optimal digestion.*

**Rejuvenate with a REAL Food Reboot**:

Excess toxins can be a cause of digestive problems for many people, causing either diarrhoea, constipation or in the case of many with IBS – both! Eliminating the foods that create inflammation in your body while replacing them with whole, nourishing and nutrient-dense foods is one of the best ways to reset your digestive and help you troubleshoot what's really going on in there. Get rid of the artificial sweeteners. These have been shown to drastically alter gut bacteria which we already know is a very important part of healthy digestion and overall health. Eliminate gluten from your diet. Gluten is a common allergen and gut irritant (even for those without gluten allergies like celiac disease). Avoid processed soy. Soy interferes with the absorption of nutrients and causes a hormone imbalance in the body when consumed in large quantities (i.e. as soy protein isolates in processed foods and beverages)

**Boost your stomach acid:**

That's right. Boost it. The truth is beloved, that high levels of hydrochloric acid, or 'stomach acid', are often not the cause of heartburn, as we've been led to believe. In fact, it's often too little stomach acid that's to blame. And so, in order for food to be released from the stomach into the small intestine, where most of the digestion and absorption of nutrients occurs, food needs to be in a liquid state. With this being the case, if you don't chew each mouthful thoroughly and you have low stomach acid,' this means your stomach needs to do more 'mechanical' digesting – or more churning and squeezing, to break the food down. As a result, this mechanical digestion takes more time, which means food is left in the stomach longer, where it can start to ferment, causing pressure to build (causing: gas and bloating). What you now have is the perfect storm; with regards to heartburn, because the increased pressure exerts force on the oesophageal sphincter (the muscle that closes the oesophagus off from the stomach); making the acid you do have, more likely to splash back up into the oesophagus.

So here are three simple ways to boost stomach acid naturally: Add freshly squeezed lemon juice to the water you drink between meals; and drink 1-2 teaspoons of raw, unfiltered apple cider vinegar in a small amount of water before each meal. And please chew your food. Chew each mouthful until it is nearly impossible to even discern what was there to start with. This may mean upwards of 15-20 chews per bite.

There is a definite craze in the health food world today, in regard to the promotion and use of digestive enzyme supplements. I have read about both the good and bad research concerning the use of them; and quite honestly, one of the most important components our body needs for healthy digestion is a good supply of digestive enzymes. And in fact, a lack of enzymes prevents us from effectively absorbing nutrients and vitamins from the foods we eat. This eventually leads to digestion problems that includes bloating, indigestion, excess gas and heartburn. We make our own enzymes, of course, however; these decline as we grow older. We can obtain enzymes such as bromelain and cellulase from eating certain raw natural foods; but unfortunately, most of us eat cooked and processed foods that contain little to no enzymes at all. This leaves us with the only option of using supplements to replenish our lost enzyme supply. If we are careful about our eating patterns and in minimising our intake of processed foods with preservatives; then the need for digestive enzyme supplements may also be reduced; however, short term use of such supplements may indeed be necessary from time to time, to assist us with food digestion, as we increase in age.

Let's face it, beloved, we've all experienced digestive problems at one time or another; and some digestive issues are harder than others to troubleshoot and fix. But many of them can be fixed with some simple adjustments to how we eat, when we eat and of course, what we eat. And also, prayer and common sense, will ensure we receive breakthrough in this area, as we seek to walk in divine health and fulfil the purposes God has for us in our lives.

# Chapter 6

## Exposing the Mysteries of Premature Death and Mental Health Conditions

My life started out quite normally by all accounts as a young girl in a Christian family. But I was always aware of the mental health issues which existed in some of the relatives that were a part of my family. I have also always been quite proud of the fact that there is a long history of pastors, evangelists and missionaries in my ancestral history; and I even have one female relative in the 1800s, that was known as "the miracle child." She performed amazingly (under God's anointing), signs, wonders, and miracles in Norway and in the Dakota Territory. And yet, there have been some of my relatives who have suffered unimaginable oppression due to demonic torment; which has attacked them in the soul realm (their minds and emotions). And so, you might ask the question, why is it that some of my relatives were walking in such victory; whilst others were walking in such defeat? This is a valid question and one I will endeavour to answer, so that you have greater understanding of Satan's plan in attacking families in this way. And by doing so, I will explain how he can cause whole bloodlines to be generationally hindered, if we do not take steps to thwart his master plan.

In my experience in pastoral counselling and deliverance ministry, I am convinced that there are specific demonic principalities that are at work upon the earth that cause both premature death and mental health disturbances in families; and especially, against families that have a specific destiny in the Kingdom of God. And these are: The Occult, Witchcraft Curses, Abuse and Immorality, Cursed Buildings and Objects, and False Religions. As a young Christian, I could not understand how men and women could be so stricken by these powerful forces; but as I entered into Christian ministry, I soon began, by the discernment of the Holy Spirit, to see what was happening more clearly. Such revelations have opened my eyes to the work that I believe has been my destiny for my entire lifetime, here on earth, so that I may help "to set the captives free," and so, that these people may go on to do the work of the Lord This ethos is written about so beautifully in (Isaiah 61:1), which says: 'The Spirit of the Sovereign LORD is on me, because the LORD has anointed me to proclaim good news to the poor.' 'And release from darkness the prisoners.'

And so, in the beginning days of my ministry, I began to look back into my own ancestral history, so that I could discover the reasons for mental health and premature death, which had existed in my own family for generations; and found that there was: alcoholism, incest and indeed immorality, and that there had been a considerable amount of foolish dabbling in the occult for at least four generations. These practices are particularly abhorrent to the Lord, and they can certainly affect us quite negatively through our bloodlines, if they are not repented of? The Bible calls drunkenness and sexual immorality, "works of the flesh" in (Galatians 5:19-22) (NASB). And in Colossians 3:1-10, we are instructed to "lay aside" such deeds; as part of the corrupt "old self" that was

crucified with Christ. Generational curses can of course be broken by stopping the cycle of sin within our bloodlines, and by confessing our sins and speaking blessings over ourselves and the next generations to come. I have used the following methods and have found them to be a successful way to go about this, as below:
1. Engage in a full surrendering of the sin
2. Confess the sins of your sinful forefathers to God, the Father
3. Be willing to fully forgive your sinful forefathers
4. Break any ungodly soul ties, which has been entered into by yourself or your forefathers.
5. Break the curse line of the demons by naming the demons, who have had a legal right to be there.
6. Verbally command the demons to leave you and your bloodlines in the name of Jesus Christ

But I would encourage you to always follow the leading of the Holy Spirit in these matters, for He is the sovereign authority in 'setting the captives free.' It is important that we understand beloved, the power in negative curses; as many cultures use the practice of cursing to cause great havoc amongst people and lands. But the Bible says in (1 John 4:4). 'But you belong to God, my dear children. You have already won a victory over those people, because the Spirit who lives in you is greater than the spirit who lives in the world.' But that does not mean that we close our eyes to negative curses or the effects of sin in our bloodlines. It simply means we recognise the hazards which we could be challenged with, and then take the necessary steps to thwart the enemy in our lives, if this type of spiritual warfare is necessary.

There are many within the Body of Christ in this day and time, who do not believe that Christians can be impacted by generational curses, witchcraft curses, or by cursed buildings or objects, or indeed by things representing false religions. But during my time, as a deliverance minister, I have seen the great disturbance that such things can cause to those I have been asked to minister to. In fact, I have seen how such things can actually cause such a spiritual blindness and hindrance to occur in a person's life; that I have had to literally stop my ministry efforts; until either the curses were identified and broken, or until the offending articles were removed from the person's home or presence, so I could proceed. May I also strongly advise that this type of deliverance should never be conducted alone; but rather with two spirit filled believers who understand the necessary steps required in order to set the oppressed person free. The name of Jesus is powerful, and every demonic spirit is aware of that power, and must submit to it; but these spirits will often try to use distraction or physical manifestations to try to distract you as a minister; from your purpose. And if a minister is alone trying to conduct deliverance ministry, he or she is particularly vulnerable in these types of circumstances.

Beloved, it is also true that such things can often only be broken by fasting and prayer, as is demonstrated in God's word in (Daniel 10:12-13), which says: Then he said to me, "Do not be afraid, Daniel, for from the first day that you set your heart on understanding this and on humbling yourself before your God, your words were heard, and I have come in response to your words. But the princes of the kingdom of Persia was withstanding me for twenty-one days, and then behold, Michael, one of the chief princes, came to help me, for I had been left there with the kings of Persia. Now I have come to give you an understanding of what will happen to your people in the latter days, for the vision pertains to the days yet future."

Beloved, in addition, I have seen remarkable stability and healing come upon those within my family, and also in those, I have ministered to, as a result of binding the oppressing demonic spirits,(at the beginning of deliverance session), as is written in (Mark 3:27): 'But no one can enter a strong man's house and plunder his goods, unless he first binds the strong man.' and then we may indeed plunder the strong man (the demon's) house, 'and engage in the above described methods to get full victory for the person being oppressed. Hallelujah! Can we get the victory for those oppressed within our families and those who have been entrusted to our ministry? Most certainly we can beloved, and furthermore, we can stop the enemy from pillaging through our bloodlines and impacting future generations, as long as, we listen to the leading of the Holy Spirit and walk free of sin.

# Chapter 7

## God's Great Cleansing Power

It is important beloved, in these days and times, that we don't underestimate the plans and devices of Satan, as he tries to bring defilement upon lands, buildings and objects. For oftentimes, such demonic strongholds can habitate in an area for decades and even centuries. In times past as a minister, I have been called upon to do prayer walking and indeed prayer explorations into buildings and certain parts of a city to discern satanic strongholds; and believe me beloved, that certain acts as well events, can indeed open up doors for demonic presences and indeed habitations to abide.

I can remember praying one time for a church building that I had been asked to cleanse. And I kept seeing in the Spirit, a young woman dressed in garments from the 19th century, and I saw her being murdered on the very plot in which the building was built upon. I don't mind telling you, that this was very unsettling for me, and yet God kept showing me this terrible vision, again and again. You see, God had shown me a row of houses on the same parcel of land, this church stood, and the Spirit of God had spoken to me "that this woman's husband had murdered her in one of those houses and had hidden her murder from the authorities," all those years ago. Well, as you might imagine, I was praying during those occasions with several of our church intercessors, so I did not immediately speak out about what the Lord had shown me. Yet, I knew in my heart of hearts, that God was showing me this terrible murder for a reason; and that because of the crime committed there, that defilement of the land had taken place. I also knew that I would need to search out proof that such a thing had occurred, in order to get the other intercessors to stand in agreement with me; and to be able to cleanse the land of this terrible act forever. This vision was so real to me, that it was like a fire shut up in my bones, and I was determined that the demonic spirit of murder would not abide on the land that God had given the people there, and I prayed for His guidance in helping me to find the proof that I needed that the event had actually taken place. Now you might say, well surely if the Power of God was moving in that church, then those demonic powers would have to flee. But beloved, the responsibility is entirely ours to take authority of such things through the Power of the Lord Jesus Christ, and then we can go in and possess the land. And an example of this is, when the Children of Israel went into the Promised Land, for they had to claim the land oftentimes by driving out their enemies first; before they could actually live and prosper in that newly acquired land, as God had ordained.

(Exodus 23:29-30) illustrates this best in God's word and says: "I will not drive them out before you in a single year, that the land may not become desolate and the beasts of the field become too numerous for you" "I will drive them out before you little by little until you become fruitful and take possession of the land "I will fix your boundary from the Red Sea to the sea of the Philistines, and from the wilderness to the River

Euphrates; for I will deliver the inhabitants of the land into your hand, and you will drive them out before you."

It is important to realise beloved, that God gives us one victory at a time, and will not give us more than we are ready for; for He wants us to depend completely on Him as we grow in our victorious walk with Him, day by day. So, I went to the library in faith, after our prayer meeting finished that day; and did the research and miraculously found in an old yellowed newspaper clipping, exactly what I was looking for. For just as the Lord had shown me, I came upon an article about a mysterious murder of a young woman in the 1870s, which had occurred in a row of terraced houses in the exact same place that the church building stood. The yellowed newspaper clipping further said: "That the young woman had been the wife of a prominent businessman; and that he had found her dead upon arriving home from his place of business."

I was so awed and honoured that God had shared such an important detail about the church land; that I kept quiet about it for a few days. During that time, God kept urging me that I must reveal the information to the pastors at the building, and to the intercessors; but the enemy kept bringing discouraging thoughts into my mind, saying, "no one will listen" and "they will think you have lost your mind." And yet, I had the proof from the library that what I had seen was entirely true; and so squaring my shoulders, I was determined to release the prophetic revelation God had given me; and I went to the church building and met with the pastors there. With admitted fear and trembling, I revealed all that God had shown me, so the land could be cleansed of the Spirit of Murder and Violence. That day, I spoke boldly of what God had shown me, and certain long-term citizens of that city were so touched, that they fell to their knees and asked forgiveness on behalf of their forefathers for the murder of that innocent woman. We also asked God to cleanse the church lands and the surrounding streets of the city from the prevailing demonic spirit of murder and violence, and praised God with music, prayers and thanksgiving, for giving us strategy and victory and drove those spirits out of our midst entirely. Joyfully, I can report in the following months, there were many signs, wonders, and miracles which occurred in that church building; and the crimes and overall violence within that part of the city decreased dramatically.

Another occurrence comes to mind, where a family in our church asked me to do prophetic exploration of their house: because their baby was very fretful during the night time hours; and they needed me to discern if indeed anything within their house was causing this ongoing issue. I prayed about their request and did feel there was something within their house that needed to be driven out, and so agreed to go with another trusted intercessor to their home to sort out the problem.

Upon entering the young family's home, I sat with the young couple in their front room; and they told us how the minute their six-month child was placed in his nursery, that he became hysterical. As a result, they had decided to let him sleep with them in their bedroom, rather than cause him such distress, and this night time dilemma had been going on for months.

I looked at the child in his mother's arms and prayed over him and did not discern anything demonic had attached itself to him.

So, I knew then, that the problem must be within the house, itself. I have learned in my many years as a minister, that children can often see things quite clearly in the spirit realm, that adults cannot see; and so, I went from room to room within the small house and asked God to show me what had unsettled the child so badly.

It did not take me long to get to the nursery, and I felt an immense grief and panic rise in my spirit when I entered the small bedroom. Immediately, the picture of a young woman being held down and raped by several men on a bed came before me, which was located in the very place that the baby's crib stood. I stifled a scream and rebuked the spirit of fear and panic that was trying to assault me; and I explained to my fellow intercessor what I saw, and she immediately said; "that although she could not see the vision God had shown me, she had discerned the spirits of murder, violence, defilement, and fear within the room."

We had left the young parents and their baby in the next room but had told them to pray and intercede and take the baby out of the house, as we explored their house. We had brought anointing oil with us, and we stood in agreement; as we prayed and rebuked every one of those spirits and commanded them to leave that nursery and the house, and to go back into dry and arid places. We then anointed the house and all its' rooms, speaking peace over it and the scripture in Romans 16:20 'The God of peace will soon crush Satan under your feet. The grace of our Lord Jesus be with you.'

You see beloved, we used the power of the Holy Spirit through the gift of discernment, and then used the authority given to us by the death and resurrection of the Lord, Jesus

Christ; and commanded those things to go and by using the Sword of the Spirit, God's Holy Word, to speak peace over that little house. You see, demons roam to and fro throughout the earth, and long to habitate if not inside humans; then close to them in land, buildings or objects; and we have full authority to command them to go, in Jesus name.

This is spoken about in the scripture (Job 1:7), where it says: The LORD said to Satan, "Where have you come from?" Satan answered the LORD, "From roaming throughout the earth, going back and forth on it." And in (Luke 9:1): "When Jesus had called the Twelve together, He gave them power and authority to drive out all demons and to cure diseases," Suffice to say, the baby did not suffer another night of oppression, and slept well from that day forwards.in that little house. Hallelujah.

Just to review beloved, upon doing Prophetic Exploration, you should:
- Pray for strategy before you go to the exploration site; and make sure you do not embark on Prophetic Exploration on your own. And you must always go with at least two of you who are strongly gifted in the power of the Holy Spirit.
- Then pray for the people at the site with the Spirit of Discernment upon your arrival.
- Make sure you bring anointing oil, as the scripture (Mark 6:13) says: 'And they were casting out many demons and were anointing with oil many sick people and healing them.'
- Then proceed with prayer by going to the four corners of the site or in the case of the house or building, into every

room and pray according to what God is showing you. You must rebuke and drive the demons out In the name of Jesus Christ and apply the blood of Jesus through use of the anointing oil, by applying the cross as protection with the anointing oil and speak peace over the house or site by using God's Word. One of the favourite scriptures I use for this purpose is from: (Leviticus 26:6): "'I will grant peace in the land, and you will lie down and no one will make you afraid. I will remove wild beasts from the land, and the sword will not pass through your country.'

# Chapter 8

## Destructive Mindsets

There is a common misconception that is being taught in the Body of Christ, that fits quite well with the world's endorsement of the humanist agenda. Many of today's Bible teachers are extolling the virtues of focusing on one's self to ensure that we walk the straight and narrow road of salvation; and while it is true that the Lord teaches us through His Word to 'examine ourselves daily,' as is written in (2 Corinthians 13:5): "Examine yourselves to see whether you are in the faith; test yourselves. Do you not realize that Christ Jesus is in you-- unless, of course, you fail the test?" Yet beloved, the truth is that too much emphasis is being given to the first part of that verse and not to the second part. For if we spend every waking hour focussing on all of our problems and on our challenges, then we will effectively close ourselves off to the still small voice of God that is leading and guiding us (which is Christ Jesus in us); and we will never reach our greater purpose in Him.

Beloved, we must learn not to judge ourselves with our own minds and emotions, which is the very core of the soul realm; but rather we must purpose in our hearts to be led, formed and shaped by the power of the Holy Spirit; and by the great love and compassion of our Living God, Jehovah, our Father. This way, our future is not limited to a continual cycle of failures, as we seek to change ourselves in our own strength. But instead, we must submit ourselves to God and His purposes; and focus upon the sacrifice that Jesus Christ made in putting every sickness, sorrow, and sin on the cross with Him, when He died and rose from the dead. We can then emerge victorious keeping our eyes fixed on that truth, which ensures we have access to the life-giving power of healing and restoration. The Lord says quite simply in His Word in (Zechariah 4:6), "This is the Word of the LORD to Zerubbabel: 'Not by might nor by power, but by my Spirit,' says the LORD Almighty. Humanism is defined: 'as a doctrine, attitude, or way of life centred on human interests or values; especially: a philosophy that usually rejects supernaturalism and stresses an individual's dignity and worth and capacity for self-realization through reason.' In effect beloved, there is a spiritual blindness that Satan propagates through the stronghold of Humanism, in both the Body of Christ, the world, and indeed many false religions around the earth today.

I have great compassion for those who are caught up in this deceptive falsehood and pray unceasingly to God to lift the spiritual blindness, which inevitably holds such people captive in both self-condemnation and perpetual defeat. I remember many years ago, when I was working as a casualty nurse in an American Emergency Hospital Department, and how one evening I encountered just such a person; who was under this foul stronghold's influence; and had resorted to desperate measures. It was about 9 pm and a middle-aged woman had been rushed into our casualty department having tried to kill herself by overdosing on sleeping pills. She was conscious when she was brought in on a stretcher by the ambulance drivers and was crying profusely at the time. The doctor that attended her that night, showed her no compassion whatsoever, and I can remember being greatly shocked at the words he spoke to her, which were "You dirty JW, why didn't you just finish the job?" As he was the senior doctor on call, I could not stop him from his cruel handling of this poor woman; but when he moved away to attend to another patient, I quickly moved to her side and tried to speak words of comfort to her, as we made preparations to pump her stomach of the lethal drugs. When we had finished the horrendous task and she was quieter later on, I went back to her side and took her hand, because I could see that she was still greatly distressed; and I asked her, "Dear, why would you do such a thing to yourself, for do you not have family that would greatly miss you, if you were gone?" And I will never forget the sad words that she spoke at the time, for as long as I live, which were: "I am a Jehovah's Witness and my leader said I am going to Hell anyway, because I have not met my quota in getting enough people into God's Kingdom." "He said my life is worthless and of no use to my brothers and sisters at the Kingdom Hall and certainly not to God." As she uttered her desperate thoughts, tears were coursing down her cheeks and I hugged her and told her: "that she was wrong, and that she was greatly loved by God and wonderfully made in His image; and I also shared with her that God loved her so much, that He sent His Only Son, Jesus, to die on the cross to set her free from sin and death, and that He wanted her to be happy and fulfilled, not so very sad."

Beloved, the stronghold that made this poor woman take such drastic steps, was in effect the demonic principality of humanism or to put it more clearly, is Satan's plan so that mankind walks in idolatry of his own thoughts and ways, which leaves out Jesus Christ's life-giving sacrifice entirely, and causes a spiral of destruction amongst humankind, which has been used as a powerful weapon by Satan since the days of the Garden of Eden. The Jehovah Witness cult, as well as, many other false religions, is definitely operating oppressively with the Spirit of Humanism, as the central focus; and sadly, controls its' people with an iron rod. In fact, this terrible stronghold leads men and women into endless wanderings away from God, which is an empty and desolate place to be. This is why I believe God is birthing in these latter days, men and women who can discern when and where this spiritual blindness exists; and through the power of God's Holy Spirit can bring a stop to it, through prayer and the teaching of the Word of God. Remember beloved, God's word says in (Romans 12:2): "Do not conform to the pattern of this world but be transformed by the renewing of your mind. Then you will be able to test and approve what God's will is--his good, pleasing and perfect will." I never saw that woman after that night; but I believe that I spoke truth to her and showed her compassion in her hour of need, as Jesus would have done. And I believe we must do the same to ensure that Jesus shines through our actions and thoughts, as we walk in His power and grace to help to set the captives free.

# Chapter 9

## Exposing Satan's Sabotaging Spirit of Division

In the many years I have been in ministry and indeed in my own life, I have seen time and time again how Satan has worked quite strategically to cause division in marriages, families, workplaces, and amongst Christians, as a whole. And it never ceases to amaze me how people are unable to detect this evil spirit at work. But I can tell you in my own case (and I am sure in many other people's); that oftentimes, I have lived life with what is known as "subjective ears and eyes," in regards to things that have been happening around me. In other words, I have been looking at life, through "rose coloured glasses" and only looking for the things I wanted to see, rather than the actual reality of what was happening in my environment.

My husband is always telling me "not everyone is like you," and he is right, for beloved, we cannot expect everyone to think and act the same way we do; and much division is caused by people placing false expectations upon other people. The Word says in (Galatians 6:1-5): 'Brothers and sisters, if someone is caught in a sin, you who live by the Spirit should restore that person gently. But watch yourselves, or you also may be tempted. Carry each other's burdens, and in this way you will fulfil the law of Christ. If anyone thinks they are something when they are not, they deceive themselves. Each one should test their own actions. Then they can take pride in themselves alone, without comparing themselves to someone else, for each one should carry their own load. Nevertheless, the one who receives instruction in the Word should share all good things with their instructor.'

Beloved, this scripture is referring to a trap Satan sets, to create "Holier than thou" Christians who walk with critical spirits towards weaker brothers and sisters, who are just learning how to walk free from strongholds and oppression in their lives. For instead of helping to carry the burden of another struggling person, as is stated in this scripture; we open up the door for the Spirit of Division to come in, by adding to their troubles and by placing false burdens upon them. Unfortunately, then the struggling person becomes so overloaded with the extra weight of their own burdens and the ones we have just added to their load; that they can never hope to rise again without a lot of intervention. Additionally, demonic spirits can then enter in and attach to the person's soul realm, (their mind and emotions), and Rejection, Depression, and Low Self-worth and even suicidal thoughts can result. And worse yet, these poor, beaten down people start to believe that they are everything that they are being criticised of, and they are terribly tormented from every side by the enemy. Beloved, this occurs in both the secular and Christian world, as Biblical principles apply when it comes to human kindness and compassion for others; regardless of the situation or the people involved. (Romans 3:2-3) says: 'We have all sinned and fallen short of the glory of God.' So this means that, although we can encourage and gently guide those we love to a place where they are free of the burdens, which is the loving arms of God, the

Father; we cannot judge or criticise them in any way. For if we do, then, we will be welcoming the Spirit of Division into the situation and our lives; and many accompanying demonic spirits which could take absolute years to be driven out.

I have pastored three churches in my lifetime and can remember speaking to a fellow pastor, who had just such a circumstance happen in his church; which ended up with his entire church being shaken so badly, that, what was once a huge, vibrant congregation dwindled down to just ten hurting people. There was a young divorced woman, who had started attending the church with her children, and sadly, from the start, there were many judgemental members of the church, who spoke against the young woman; because of her being divorced. She was a beautiful and vivacious young woman, who had been a Christian since her childhood; and had fallen victim to an adulterous husband, who had left her for a woman that owned a bar in the same town. As time wore on, the women of the church refused to allow her to bond with them and even called her things like "Jezebel," (who was a harlot queen in the Old Testament). The young woman had come into the church innocently enough, with pure intentions of building relationships with a new church family to support her through the difficult time in her life. But instead, all she received was judgement and criticism. Six months passed with constant criticism and rejection being directed towards the young woman from the church congregation; and as a result, the Spirit of Division was fully entrenched within the church. The Pastor and his ministry team had tried to show the woman compassion, in spite of the congregations' low opinion of her; but it wasn't long before the vulnerable, young woman was so desperate for validation and support in her struggles; that she formed an emotional attachment and an ungodly soul tie with the church's young, married youth pastor, and inevitably; sexual sin occurred. This was very tragic; because the young woman had become exactly what the church members had proclaimed her to be in her desperation; and Satan had not only brought down the young woman and the youth pastor; but the entire church too. Beloved, that Pastor's church operated exactly the opposite to God's Biblical principles, which allowed the terrible devastation that took place there. So, in order to keep the door to the Spirit of Division firmly closed, it is important to remember that we must live as Jesus did; and extend love and compassion to all those who are hurting, for there is healing and peace in such Godly love.

As a nurse, I can tell you that some wounds can look pretty horrific at first, when a person has suffered injury or has just come back from surgery. But that doesn't mean that as a nurse, I can just turn a blind eye to the wound and say: "Well, that person should have been more careful or lived a healthier lifestyle and then they wouldn't have had that wound at all." For beloved, my duty as a nurse is to clean the wound and change the dressing each day; so that no infection sets in, and so that the person's wound heals properly." God says in his Word in (Psalm 147:3) that 'He heals the broken-hearted and binds up their wounds.' And so, we as His followers must ensure we do the same in our hearts, attitudes and actions towards the broken-hearted; or we will help to propagate sin and inevitably, demonic strongholds will take root in our lives and environments. We are now in the latter days, beloved, and God is calling us to bring the lost into the His Kingdom, regardless of the ugly wounds they may carry. So, let us defeat the sabotaging tactics of Satan and firmly block the Spirit of Division from taking control of our lives. Hallelujah!

# Chapter 10

## The Truth About Witches, Ghosts, Poltergeists, and Demonic Manifestations

In much of the western world and indeed in many Christian denominations that exist today, there is a lot of denial when it comes to the supernatural realm; and many people attribute such things to the 'world of make believe' or indeed Hollywood. I am of the opinion, that this mindset is either because of spiritual blindness, or a demonic spirit called the Spirit of Fear or perhaps, both. Such things can render mankind virtually powerless against an occultist spirit or witchcraft curse: and if the man or woman of God does not walk in the full authority of Jesus Christ and drive these things out through declarations and prayers; it can cause generational curses and indeed, sickness and premature death to abide in a family's bloodlines for a very long time.

Beloved, we are not glorifying these things by speaking of them, for we must understand the nature of ourselves in relation to the supernatural, and how it all works. We are inquisitive by nature and most of us are seekers of truth. But I would caution you, that there is a sort of fascination that mankind has with supernatural things, for we are all born with three parts of ourselves, the body, soul, and spirit, and our spirits long to commune with God. And if we cannot find Him due to numerous reasons, then we will settle for a counterfeit to fulfil that need.

You can hardly sit around a campfire these days without hearing ghost stories or people bringing up accounts of angelic visitations that they have experienced during their lives. But there is very little teaching in the church today, about familiar spirits or ghosts or poltergeists, or about the purposes of angels in the heavens and on the earth. Familiar spirits or ghosts are mentioned numerous times in the Bible, and usually in conjunction with mediums. One such example is in Leviticus 20:6 which says: "I will also turn against those who commit spiritual prostitution by putting their trust in mediums or in those who consult familiar spirits. I will cut them off from the community."

Beloved, God is warning His people in this scripture to not become involved with witchcraft or familiar spirits; for these things are born of Satan and mediums or psychics, work directly with demonic spirits; who can take on the form of a loved one, (or anything they please) to propagate a lie and create a soul tie with a human and themselves. Because once a person's soul realm has communed with a demonic spirit, then this creates a portal for horrendous attacks from Satan and his cohorts.

Remember beloved, that Satan was cast out of the heavenlies; because of his great sin of pride and stubbornness and his rebellion against God. And if we are consorting with mediums or familiar spirits, then we are linking ourselves with them and their rebellion against God. (1 Samuel 15:23) says: 'Rebellion is as the sin of witchcraft, and stubbornness and as bad as worshiping idols. So, because you have rejected the command of the LORD, He has rejected you as king."

In the Bible, King Saul is described, as a very troubled man; much given to tormenting spirits and depression. So much so, that he often had to be calmed by bringing David to court to play beautiful music for him in order to bring him to a place of peace. I believe this is because Saul often rebelled against God, and had so much demonic oppression, that he was confused and could not hear the voice of God for himself.

And so instead, he would either rely upon the words of the priest Samuel, or whatever source he could find to direct his steps. Now mediums and sorcery had been banned in the land of Israel during that time; but there is a story in the Bible which tells of Saul approaching the Witch of Endor, a well-known medium of the day. who worked with familiar spirits, to bring Samuel back from the dead, to give him advice in: (1 Samuel 28:7), which says: When Saul inquired of the LORD, the LORD did not answer him, either by dreams or by Urim or by the prophets. Then Saul said to his servants, "Seek for me a woman who is a medium, that I may go to her and inquire of her." And his servants said to him: "Behold there is a woman called the 'Witch of Endor,' Then Saul disguised himself by putting on other clothes, and went, he and two men with him, and they came to the woman by night; and he said, "Conjure up for me, please, and bring up for me whom I shall name to you."... Now beloved, such open rebellion was a terrible thing, especially for a king appointed over God's people. And Saul knew he was going against God in visiting the 'Witch of Endor, 'for advice, yet. he disguised himself and did it anyway. And as a result, when the Witch was able to bring Samuel back, he received a terrible rebuke and prediction for the future and in the end tragically he killed himself.

Beloved, it is very important that we do not "play with fire," and put ourselves in the position that we are aligning ourselves with Satan and his demonic spirits... by communing with them through consulting mediums, using tarot cards, or even reading horoscopes. Because such things can cause us to be in rebellion against God and have tremendous curses and indeed tormenting spirits come upon our lives. Also, we should not in my opinion, watch films or play video games that propagate or glorify witchcraft or ghosts; because of the likelihood of us opening ourselves up to the attacks of the enemy.

In addition, I am convinced that demonic spirits habitate in objects that represent the occult or witchcraft, or also, can abide in locations where false religion or witchcraft objects have been or where occultist actions have taken place. This is why we must be so careful about the things we come in contact with on every level. This is not to make you fearful beloved; but rather to help you understand the seriousness of this stronghold. Of course, if you do come upon such demonic articles or places, prophetic exploration can take place and your location sanctified through the power of the Holy Spirit and under the authority of the Lord Jesus Christ. And in a later chapter, I include a powerful declaration prayer to ensure that your houses or buildings are cleansed, and all demonic spirits are driven out.

Beloved, because Spiritual House Cleansing is not a commonly taught subject in many churches, it is important to know five biblical principles before you embark on such a venture.

I can assure you that such wisdom on the subject will genuinely enhance the effectiveness of the cleansing. In fact, in truth, these five principles are actually more relevant to us as individual believers; rather than, the physical structures we seek to cleanse. But nevertheless, need to be considered; because we are the house or dwelling place of the Lord, in which the Holy Spirit's Power gives us instruction, as we take authority in the name of Jesus over the enemy in such circumstances.

1. **Spiritual Warfare:** Demonic spirits desire to enter, disrupt, cause confusion, inhabit and multiply in people as well as places. They do this when there is a legal right given to them. A legal right is simply a way of saying that a person has authorized the demon to operate in their lives. A good example of this is (Ephesians 4:27): "and do not give the devil an opportunity." The King James uses the word "place" instead of opportunity. Beloved, as mentioned in previous chapters, people can indeed give a legal right for a demonic spirit to attach or invade or torment them. This can occur in their homes, offices or other areas of their life. And Christians should in no way feel they are exempt from this.

2. **The Authority of Believers.** When the seventy disciples returned, they commented "Lord, even the demons are subject to us in your name" and Jesus replied "I was watching Satan fall from heaven like lightning. Behold, I have given you authority to tread upon serpents and scorpions, and over all the power of the enemy, and

nothing shall by any means injure you. Nevertheless, do not rejoice in this, that the spirits are subject to you, but rejoice that your names are recorded in heaven" (Luke 10:17b – 20 NASB). Beloved, without a doubt, God's Word proclaims that we, as believers; have authority over demonic spirits and over all the work of the enemy. We also have power when baptized in the Holy Spirit as mentioned in (Acts 1:4-8). However, we would be wise to follow the instructions that Jesus gave to the seventy disciples and "guard ourselves so that we don't become prideful or focus on the wrong things." In addition, it is important to remember that no one has authority except we, as believers; to cast out demonic spirits. The seven sons of Sceva, learned this the hard way, when demonic spirits overpowered them to the point that they were left entirely naked and wounded from the assault (Acts 19:14-17). Make sure beloved, that you know who you are in Christ, before you confront the enemy.

3. **Spiritual Cleansing.** In regards to the actual act of spiritual cleansing, the Old Testament has many examples of cleansing, but I believe the best example can be found in (Matthew 12:22-28): "Then they brought Him (Jesus), a demon-possessed man; who was blind and mute, and Jesus healed him, so that he could both talk and see. All the people were astonished and said, "Could this be the Son of David?" But when the Pharisees heard this, they said, "It is only by Beelzebub, the prince of demons, which this fellow drives out demons." Jesus knew their thoughts and said to them, "Every kingdom

divided against itself will be ruined, and every city or household divided against itself will not stand. If Satan drives out Satan, he is divided against himself. How then can his kingdom stand? And if I drive out demons by Beelzebub, by whom do your people drive them out? So then, they will be your judges. But if it is by the Spirit of God that I drive out demons, then the Kingdom of God has come upon you. Beloved, it is important to remember that light cannot habitate with darkness, and if we have houses, buildings, or indeed bodies; that are divided between God and the evil one, Satan; then such things must be cleansed and put right by driving all evil influences out, in Jesus's name. Amen!

4. **Dedication and the Anointing**. It was a common practice throughout the Bible to dedicate and anoint both people and things unto the Lord. Anointing and dedicating is simply a way to set a person or thing apart for God and His service (Gen. 28:18; 1 Kings 1:16; Ex. 28:41, 29:7; Lev. 8:12-30).

5. **God's Presence**. Beloved, anytime a demonic spirit is driven out from a person or place; it is hugely important that it be filled with the presence of the Lord. For these evil spirits cannot come back to live in a vessel that is filled with the loving, presence of the Lord. However, it is important for you to remind the person or owner of the building, that if unbelief comes in or if wilful disobedience occurs then the demon spirits can come back seven times worse.

This is shown in the scripture (Luke 11:24-25): "When the unclean spirit goes out of a man, it passes through waterless places seeking rest, and not finding any, it says 'I will return to my house from which I came.' And when it comes, it finds it swept and put in order. Then it goes and takes along seven other spirits more evil than itself and they go in and live there.

Beloved, in the case of a demonic article, like a painting or sculpture, sometimes; it is just best to get rid of the offending articles altogether, rather than risk temptation, sin, or demonic open doors. God's Word says in (Mark 9: 43): "If your hand causes you to stumble, cut it off. It is better for you to enter life maimed than with two hands to go into hell, where the fire never goes out." Remember, God loves you and only wants you to have an oppression-free life, whilst walking in victory; as you follow His instructions. Let your spirit commune with God and no one else, and you will find both peace and joy is prevalent in your life. Praise God!

# Chapter 11

## Cooperating with the Holy Spirit

Beloved, there is a key Biblical principle that you would be wise to embrace in order to remain free from demonic oppression and sickness; and that is the act of cooperating with the Holy Spirit. Such cooperation oftentimes takes faith coupled with perseverance; but will reap great rewards, if we can maintain this important mindset and behaviour. In the book of Mark, there are marvellous examples of this principle; as Jesus interacted with suffering people who demonstrated this key life skill. But let us first examine the Trinity and why the Holy Spirit can work to lead, guide, heal and deliver us from evil; as He empowers Christians to act as His conduits for His power in these latter days. Beloved, God the Father created all things in the heavens and the earth, and Jesus Christ is His only Son, who sacrificed Himself upon the cross, more than 2000 years ago. But to help you understand the third entity in the Godhead, the Holy Spirit, let us go to (John 16:7), which says: "But very truly I tell you, it is for your good that I am going away. For unless I go away, the Advocate will not come to you; but if I go, I will send Him to you." In this passage, Jesus was talking to the disciples about the Holy Spirit, who has been called in God's Word, the advocate, helper, and comforter for us, God's children. Jesus knew that after His resurrection from the dead, that He would be going to Heaven to join His Father;

and that through His death on the cross, He had ensured that we would have access to His authority and have eternal life. And He also knew that we would need access to power from on high, in order to remain victorious in all aspects of our lives here on earth. So in other words, God, the Father is the Creator of the Heavens and the Earth, Jesus Christ is His Only Begotten Son and our stamp of authority, and The Holy Spirit is our comforter and friend, who leads and guides us and gives us power to not only ensure victory in our own lives; but also, will assist us to bring about the same victory in others. Beloved Jesus said in (John 14:12), "Very truly I tell you, whoever believes in me will do the works I have been doing, and they will do even greater things than these, because I am going to the Father." In this scripture, He is referring to the mighty power of God that we have access to, in order to not only understand and implement God's Word; but also to be able to walk successfully in the giftings God has imparted to us from the very moment of our creation.

Beloved, this means when each person accepts Jesus Christ as His Savior, as the first part of this verse indicates, that there is a measure God's Holy Spirit power that is imparted to him or her. But there is also a greater impartation that Christians can have access to as well, called the "Baptism of the Holy Spirit." This is spoken of in (Acts 11:16), which says: Then I remembered what the Lord had said: 'John baptized with water, but you will be baptized with the Holy Spirit.' Beloved, more empowerment from on High is a very good thing, and I would encourage you to seek after this impartation. For it will help you to hear God's voice more clearly and also, to walk in the fullness of the Spiritual giftings, that God has given you.

In the Book of Mark, Jesus performed many miracles and drove out demons in numerous towns throughout Judea, and always, the key element to each miracle or healing was the faith and belief the people had in the power of the Holy Spirit working through Jesus. One example was when He had forgiven a paralytic his sins in Mark Chapter 2. Jesus had discerned that the reason the man was crippled was because of a sin condition which had opened up the door for demonic oppression, hence; the spirit of infirmity had caused him to be paralyzed. Jesus then said to the paralytic "Son, your sins or forgiven." For He had seen the great faith that the paralytic man and his friends had shown to get the oppressed man in front of Him, because they had lowered him from the roof to get past the crowds. And yet sadly, the teachers of the Hebrew Law were still there questioning His authority amongst themselves. Jesus could see into their hearts and responded: "Why do you reason these things in your hearts, (soul realm)?" You see beloved, Jesus knew that these teachers of the law could not possibly understand His authority, or the power of the Holy Spirit with their own minds or emotions; and yet, He had seen faith and cooperation exercised by the paralytic man and his friends; and so, He told the man to "take up his mat and walk" and that is exactly what he did. Praise God!

Faith and belief in God's grace and power are absolute prerequisites, if we are going to cooperate with the Holy Spirit and get breakthrough in every area of our lives. Beloved, if we do not have these key mindsets, and try to reason about God's ways or for that matter, why such trials have come upon us, we are actually opening ourselves up to a humanistic mind-set, which can in turn, open up the door to all kinds of destructive thoughts, and even worse; we will be cooperating with Satan and his minions, not the Holy Spirit. God longs to bring breakthrough and freedom to His people; but such things are severely hindered, if unbelief abounds in a person or location. This is clearly shown in Mark 6, when Jesus went to His hometown, Nazareth, and it says: "Jesus left there, and went to His hometown, accompanied by His disciples. When the Sabbath came, He began to teach in the synagogue, and many who heard Him were amazed.

"Where did this man get these things?" they asked. "What's this wisdom that has been given Him?" "What are these remarkable miracles He is performing? "Isn't this the carpenter?" "Isn't this Mary's son and the brother of James, Joseph, Judas and Simon?" "Aren't His sisters here with us?" "And they took offense at Him." Jesus said to them, "A prophet is not without honour except in his own town, among his relatives and in his own home." He could not do any miracles there, except lay his hands on a few sick people and heal them. He was amazed at their lack of faith.

Beloved, to stay free from oppression and sickness and in order for us to be prepared as mighty men and woman of God, to bring in a great harvest into God's kingdom, we must have faith and learn to cooperate with the Holy Spirit. The Word says in (Romans 1:17): "For the gospel reveals the righteousness of God that comes by faith from start to finish, just as it is written: "The righteous will live by faith."

# Chapter 12

## The Power of Positive Confession

It is important as men and women of God, that we understand the power that is generated from the spoken word. (Proverbs 18:21), says: "The tongue has the power of life and death, and those who love it will eat its' fruit." Spoken blessings and curses can result in immense breakthrough or immense damage; as is backed up by this Old Testament verse. This is because when our words are spoken in line with Biblical principles and under the authority of the Lord Jesus Christ; and when we are empowered by the direction of the Holy Spirit, miraculous blessings can be the wonderful result. But alternatively, if words are spoken against Biblical principles and are uttered with hatred, jealousy, or lust, then curses through demonic oppression or poor health can be the sad result.

Bold declarations according to God's Word can stop the enemy in his tracks, as long as, we work under the authority of the name of Jesus. The Apostle Paul in Romans, Chapter 8, made several bold declarations which changed the very life and heart of the New Testament Church. These declarations were given to Paul by the Holy Spirit, and not only did they give hope to Christians; but they gave men and women of God, a better insight of God, the Father, and His great love for us.

They are as follows:
- V. 1 There is no condemnation for those who are in Christ Jesus
- V. 9 you no longer have to be controlled by the sinful nature, but by the Spirit
- V. 14 those who are led by the Spirit of God are Sons of God
- V. 16 the Spirit assures us that we are God's Children and heirs of His rich blessing
- V. 18 our present suffering is nothing compared with the glory that will be revealed in us
- V. 23 we look forward to Heaven where our full adoption as Sons, will be completed
- V. 26 the Spirit is given by God to help us when we have trouble praying
- V. 28 in every circumstance God is working for the good of those who love God
- V. 29 The believer is foreknown, predestined, called, justified and glorified.

It is important to understand beloved that Satan wants to cause spiritual blindness to come upon God's people; so that they are so confused and oppressed, that they cannot hope to overcome their own problems, much less; bring compassion and blessing to someone else. And we, as humans, do tend to be inundated with all sorts of emotions and negative thoughts, when we are going through trials. This results in negative words that we say over and over again, as we give in to sickness or indeed other battles. A good example I can give from my own life is in regard to a season where I had problems with my right foot. I had developed a very painful condition called 'Morton's Neuroma.' and had two of them causing such severe symptoms, that I had to use a crutch to help with my mobility and to get around. And beloved, I would then reinforce the condition by always talking about how bad the symptoms were; and also, that "I had inherited my bad feet from my mother." And after about a year God showed me through His Word; how my negative words were making the season of sickness in my foot even longer. Ephesians 4:29 says: 'Let no corrupting talk come out of your mouths, but only such as is good for building up, as fits the occasion, that it may give grace to those who hear.' Now beloved, we do not need to walk in condemnation, if we do become ill or have certain poor health conditions; because such things could have come upon us for any number of reasons. But we don't have to make matters worse by speaking curses over ourselves either. Because it is no good praying for God's healing power and then in the next breath, showing unbelief and a lack of faith in His ability to sort the health problem out by speaking negative words. (2 Corinthians 4:13): says: "We having the same spirit of faith, according as it is written, I believed, and therefore have I spoken; we also believe, and therefore speak." And so, from this verse, we can deduce that our spoken word can inspire our spirits to have faith, which can then bring about the miracle working power of the Holy Spirit. With my own foot problem, I decided to start working in cooperation with the Holy Spirit; and stopped speaking curses over my foot, and although, I did have to undergo surgery, my recovery time was greatly reduced; just because I started speaking blessing and believed that God's healing power could actually bring healing to my foot.

Now beloved, this is God's biblical principle not my own, and I believe can be applied to any area of oppression in our lives, whether it is sickness, addiction, or poverty; but remember that God is sovereign and will decide when and how the victory comes. Also, you must ensure that you have changed your negative behaviour, for God will simply not bring breakthrough, if we are showing a lack of faith. But I can tell you, that God is a compassionate Father, and nothing is "written in stone;" and if we cry out to Him, He will answer us in our distress.

Word curses also can originate from others speaking or praying against us. These are called "witchcraft curses or prayers," and can cause sickness, tragedy or circumstances to come against us. And today in certain countries around the world, there are even witch doctors and shamans, who specialise in this, and put curses on people through demonic power for money. In fact, in some cultures "voodoo" is practiced. This includes the practice of sticking pins in a doll made in the image of the person, usually with some of the person's hair. There are other hateful witchcraft and satanic rituals that work in much the same way; but I won't go into the details of such rituals, so I don't have to give any more attention to wickedness, than I absolutely have to.

Beloved, please note, that this does not mean that every difficult circumstance we go through is because of a word curse; and as mentioned before in a previous chapter; sometimes God will allow a season to stretch a bit longer to teach us something. But if God shows us, that a word curse is the root of the problem; then we must examine our behaviour and rectify it, by repenting and changing our negativity in order to get the breakthrough we need. And if it comes from another source, then we have the power and authority through the Lord Jesus Christ to break the word curse and its' power over us. (Luke 9:1): says: 'When Jesus had called the Twelve together, He gave them power and authority to drive out all demons and to cure diseases.'

In today's world, there are still fully operating curses in the lives of many Christians; because they are partaking in some level of sin, which God considers open rebellion towards Him and His commands. But beloved, if we walk in covenant with Him, nothing by any means can hurt us, as is written in (Luke 10:19): "I have given you authority to trample on snakes and scorpions and to overcome all the power of the enemy; nothing will harm you." By making a declaration that you will separate yourself from sin, and by repenting of it; and then by speaking forth that you forgive those who have spoken against you, you will be showing the love and compassion towards all those that have caused you pain and thereby imitating the ways of God. This will cancel the curse entirely beloved, for such actions can only release the power of God into the circumstances every time, as He honours His covenant with us, and causes the enemy to flee. Hallelujah!

# Chapter 13

## The Relationship Between Idolatry and Demons

With the attractions of the world so plentiful and the importance placed on money and status in today's society, more aspired to than ever, it is easy to see how Satan can use such things to get the priorities of human beings all mixed up. Also, with the demonic stronghold of humanism convincing men and women everywhere they look, to place their own desires first over everything and everyone, a door is then opened very wide for Idolatry to be a behaviour pattern that can consequently lead to addictions, broken relationships, and all sorts of destructive circumstances. (Deuteronomy 32:16–17) states, "They stirred God to jealousy with strange gods; and with abominations they provoked Him to anger." "They sacrificed to demons that were no gods, and to gods they had never known, to new gods that had come recently, whom your fathers had never dreaded."

This passage associates pagan gods with "demons" and warns God's people not to be involved with idolatry. In fact, the Hebrew text here uses, what is called: 'synonymous parallelism,' in which two or more lines communicate the same idea using different words. In this case, the parallels include "strange gods" and "demons that were no gods." Grammatically, the demons and the foreign gods are the same.

The text clearly connects pagan worship with evil spirits. The false gods are in contrast with the one true God, the "Rock" in verses 15 and 17.

(Leviticus 17:7) adds another important connection, and says: "They shall no more offer their sacrifices to demons, after whom they have played the harlot" In this verse, it is talking about demons which were the other gods which were worshiped by the surrounding cultures. Again, demons are equated with pagan gods in this passage.

It is no coincidence that demonic activity is associated with religions that embrace a multitude of gods and goddesses. A desire to have supernatural contact with the "spirit world" often focuses people on supernatural power apart from the power God offers through a relationship with Jesus Christ; and His Holy Spirit. Without a doubt, the devil desires to be worshiped, which is clearly shown in (Matthew 4:9), when Jesus was being tested in the wilderness, and he asked Jesus to bow down to him by saying: "All this I will give you, if you will bow down and worship me."

Also, demons most assuredly teach false doctrine, which is spoken about in 1 Timothy 4:1, which says: "The Spirit clearly says that in later times, some will abandon the faith and follow deceiving spirits and things taught by demons." The truth is beloved, that those who worship false gods or spend an inordinate amount of time focussing on things other than God, wittingly or unwittingly, are pledging their allegiance to evil spirits, who desire to usurp God's rightful place in their hearts; and to destroy as many people as possible in the process.

Modern day idols, which we put before God, may be any number of things, however; the Spirit of Mammon or

Materialism is certainly at the top of the list. Quite often, people worship at the altar of materialism; because it feeds their need to build their egos through the acquisition of more "stuff." And sadly, as their homes are then filled with all manner of possessions to reflect their outward success; the inside of their homes are often filled with sadness and demonic oppression, because their focus has been on getting rich and not upon being in relationship with God. They buy, more and more possessions, in hopes that such purchases will fill the emptiness that only God can fill, and a great deal of these possessions aren't' even paid for yet, as people buy them on credit. These types of purchases then open up the door for the Spirit of Poverty to oppress human beings, as such debt increases from year to year.

Most of these possessions have a "planned obsolescence" built into them, (which is a great moneymaking scheme used by manufacturers, as they spend millions in advertising campaigns, extolling the virtues of the newest models coming out, such as in mobile phones); making the purchased items useless in no time, and then we rush out to buy the newest item, garment or gadget, and the whole process starts all over again. Beloved, this insatiable appetite for more, better, and newer stuff is nothing more than 'covetousness.' And the tenth commandment tells us not to fall victim to coveting and says: "You shall not covet your neighbour's house." "You shall not covet your neighbour's wife, or his manservant or maidservant, his ox or donkey, or anything that belongs to your neighbour" (Exodus 20:17). In this commandment beloved, God doesn't want to ban us from things that could make our life more comfortable or happy. But He is very aware that we can never be happy indulging our materialistic desires; because it is Satan's trap to keep our focus on ourselves and not upon Him.

Another, modern-day idol is our own pride and ego. This often takes the form of obsession with careers and jobs. In fact, millions of men and increasingly more women; spend 60-80 hours a week working. Even on the weekends and during vacations, our laptops are humming and our minds are whirling with thoughts of how to make our businesses more successful; or how to get that promotion, or how to get the next pay rise, or how to close the next deal. In the meantime, our children are starving for attention and love; and our focus upon God is abandoned altogether. You see beloved, we fool ourselves into thinking we are doing it for our families, to give them a better life. But the truth is, we are doing it for ourselves, to increase our self-esteem by appearing more successful in the eyes of the world. Beloved, this is folly; because all of our labours and accomplishments will be of no use to us, after we die. And neither will the admiration of the world be of any use; because these things just do not have any eternal value.

As King Solomon put it, "For a man may do his work with wisdom, knowledge and skill, and then he must leave all he owns to someone who has not worked for it." "This too is meaningless and a great misfortune." "What does a man get for all the toil and anxious striving with which he labours under the sun?" "For all of his days, his work is pain and grief; and even at night his mind does not rest." "This too is meaningless" (Ecclesiastes 2:21-23).

Another type of modern idolatry is when we worship mankind through naturalism and the power of science. Many of us cling to the illusion that we are lords of our world; and build our self-esteem to godlike proportions. In fact, we reject God's Word and His description of how He created the heavens and the earth, and we accept the nonsense of atheistic evolution and naturalism. Furthermore, we embrace the goddess of environmentalism and fool ourselves into thinking we can preserve the earth indefinitely; when God has declared that this current age will have an end, as is written in (2 Peter 3:10–13).: "But the day of the Lord will come like a thief." "The heavens will disappear with a roar; the elements will be destroyed by fire, and the earth and everything in it will be laid bare." "Since everything will be destroyed in this way, what kind of people ought you to be?" "You ought to live holy and godly lives as you look forward to the day of God and speed its coming." "That day will bring about the destruction of the heavens by fire, and the elements will melt in the heat." "But in keeping with his promise we are looking forward to a new heaven and a new earth, the home of righteousness." As this passage clearly states beloved, our focus should not be on worshiping the environment; but rather on living holy lives; as we wait eagerly for the return of our Lord and Saviour; and He alone deserves our worship.

Finally, and perhaps most destructively, we worship at the altar of self-aggrandizement or the fulfilment of the self to the exclusion of all others; and their needs and desires. This manifests itself in self-indulgence, through alcohol, drugs, and food. Those in affluent countries have unlimited access to alcohol, drugs (prescription drug use is at an all-time high, even among children), and food. Obesity rates in the U.S. have skyrocketed, and childhood diabetes brought on by overeating is at epidemic proportions.

The self-control we so desperately need is spurned in our insatiable desire to eat, drink, and medicate more and more. Sadly, we resist any effort to get us to curb our appetites, and we are determined to make ourselves the god of our lives. This has its' origin in the Garden of Eden where Satan tempted Eve to eat of the tree with the words "you will be like God" (Genesis 3:5). This has been man's desire ever since, to be god, and as we have seen, the worship of self is the basis of all modern idolatry.

Beloved, all idolatry of self has at its' core the three lusts which are found in (1 John 2:16): "For all that is in the world, the lust of the flesh, and the lust of the eyes, and the pride of life, is not of the Father, but is of the world." And if we are to escape modern day idolatry, we have to admit that it is rampant in our lives and reject it in all of its' forms. It is not of God, but of Satan, and in it we will never find fulfilment. And to think otherwise is a very great lie, and the same one Satan has been telling since he first lied to Adam and Eve. Sadly, we are still falling for it. Even more sadly, many churches are propagating it, in the preaching of the health, wealth, and prosperity gospel built on the idol of self-esteem.

But the truth is, we will never find happiness focusing on ourselves. Our hearts and minds must be centred on God and on others. This is why when asked what is the greatest commandment, Jesus replied, "Love the Lord your God with all your heart and with all your soul and with all your mind" (Matthew 22:37). When we love the Lord and others with everything that is in us, beloved, then there will be no room in our hearts for idolatry.

# Chapter 14

## How Purpose Promotes Our Wellbeing

There has been an almost casting off of all works by many people in the Body of Christ, in the last few decades; and numerous preachers have spoken about the fact: "That works alone will not get us into the Kingdom of God." And yet, whilst it is true that we cannot earn the gift of eternal life or the grace of God through works, it is important to keep in mind that certain works are imperative in order for us to fulfil God's great commission and to ensure our wellbeing. So, what is God's great commission and how does it affect our health and wellbeing? In (Matthew 28:16-20); it states:" Then the eleven disciples went to Galilee, to the mountain where Jesus had told them to go." ""When they saw Him, they worshiped Him; but some doubted." "Then Jesus came to them and said, "All authority in heaven and on earth has been given to me". "Therefore, go and make disciples of all nations, baptizing them in the name of the Father and of the Son and of the Holy Spirit," "and teaching them to obey everything I have commanded you." "And surely, I am with you always, to the very end of the age."

Beloved, these important verses speak of our purpose and destiny upon this earth. Jesus has given us His authority, so that "we may make disciples of all nations, baptizing them in the name of the Father and of the Son and of the Holy Spirit" and so that we can "teach them a victorious walk in Him" for eternity, and introduce a 'Kingdom of God Culture.' These verses are speaking about a hope which transcends time, and the cares of this life; and about a hope that will remain constant for all eternity. And this beautiful hope and security we can also bestow upon others, as a free gift. Beloved, (Proverbs 13:12), says: "Hope deferred makes the heart sick, but a longing fulfilled is a tree of life." You see, mankind is made in God's image, inside and out, and just as our Father in heaven; is a God of order and purpose, we as His children are the happiest when we are also walking with order and purpose, as we fulfil the destiny that He has ordained for us.

Remember beloved, there is God's perfect will for our lives and then there is His permissive will; and if we make a series of wrong decisions in disobedience to God's perfect will for our lives, He will not forsake us, for He loves us dearly. But it may take longer for us to fulfil His will, if we end up taking a path that allows Satan to play havoc with our lives. For it is important to realise, that even if we do alter our lives through wrong decisions in life, that God is always there ready and waiting for us, and will give us that wonderful hope, when we repent and come back into fellowship with Him.

In a previous chapter, I mentioned how Paul made declarations given to him by the Holy Spirit, and one particular declaration clarifies God's wonderful master plan for us, as His children in (Romans, Chapter 8:29-30): "For those God foreknew, He also predestined to be conformed to the image of His Son, that He might be the firstborn among many brothers and sisters." "And those He predestined, He also called, those He called, He also justified, those He justified, He also glorified." Beloved, a purposeful state of mind is of extreme importance, if we are to succeed in this life and be happy. God has created us like this, and even renowned mental health experts of the day, agree such purpose in our lives is wholly necessary, for us, as human beings to ensure our wellbeing. In fact, a recent article in an internationally recognised psychology publication said: "The need for purpose is one of the defining characteristics of human beings." "Human beings crave purpose and suffer serious psychological difficulties; when they don't have it." "Purpose is a fundamental component of a fulfilling life."

And as Christians, we can achieve the purpose we have been created for, by loving people through exhibiting God's great gifts of compassion; and by reaching out to the oppressed and hurting multitudes in love. Such actions reflect the very essence, heart, and life of Jesus Christ. Beloved, I will reiterate, God's great commission is our destiny, as we share His love, hope, and compassion under the authority of the Lord, Jesus Christ through our words, as well as, our actions. And such focus on helping others, will keep us from falling into the trap of only focussing upon ourselves; as we rise up as an end time army of God, carrying out God's will in this dark, and oppressive world.

Unconditional love, expressed through words and actions, can ensure, a two-fold outcome, as both the giver of the love through the gift of Christ like compassion and the receivers of this marvellous outpouring; feel the touch of the Holy Spirit in a very tangible and powerful way. It is my firm belief, that it is the combination of this heartfelt love, (that only God can provide through His people to a dying world); that will truly cause a great transformation to occur in the unsaved populations of mankind across the earth.

For there can be no denying God's loving intentions, as people are shown love and compassion through faith, love and works. In fact, the Lord once showed me a vision of how our loving, Father God, longs to place the wedding band upon the finger of His glorious Bride in the Body of Christ. And I saw in the vision, 'a beautiful woman dressed in an exquisite wedding gown and smiling sweetly and waiting in expectation for her bridegroom to place the wedding band upon her finger.' 'And yet, when she raised her hand to receive the wonderful honour, I saw that her hands were missing entirely'. Then the Lord spoke to me and said: "My people have every good intention; but the workers are few for my harvest, because the enemy is stealing time and blinding my people, so that they are only focussed upon themselves." "And I greatly desire that the hands of My Bride be restored, so that My great work can go forth by My Spirit." "For it will only be My Remnant, that will put their whole hearts into the works of My great harvest; and will see the fulfilment of My outpouring and My glory in the latter days."

Beloved, Jesus personified compassion when He walked upon the earth and (Matthew 9:36), says: "When He saw the crowds, He had compassion on them; because they were harassed and helpless, like sheep without a shepherd." And you might ask me, but Leisa, what does this have to do with being healthy? And I would answer you by saying: "Everything," for heart health should be at the very core of our spiritual beings. Beloved, God knows us better than anyone and He knows that if we have pure hearts and pure minds, and we are walking in love; as we show compassion and help towards others, that this will ensure our own wellbeing, as peace and harmony and great blessings (which includes divine health) overtakes our lives.

Because beloved, if we are living according to God's biblical principles, whilst seeking to emulate Jesus Christ, our Saviour, then God will ensure we are safeguarded for His purposes here on Earth, as is written in John 3:16-17 "For God so loved the world, that He gave His only begotten Son, that whoever believes in Him shall not perish, but have eternal life, for God did not send the Son into the world, to judge the world; but that the world might be saved through Him." And Jeremiah 33:6 further says: "'Nevertheless, I will bring health and healing to them; I will heal my people and will let them enjoy abundant peace and security." Hallelujah!

# Chapter 15

## How to Identify Spiritual Oppression

Beloved, a large part of our wellbeing has to do with our mindsets. Remember our minds are a part of our soul realm, which the enemy often attacks through demonic oppression. One such spirit, is called the spirit of witchcraft; which is a powerful spirit which can often manipulate human beings in a horribly destructive manner. Most modern day people living in the Western World, can only picture witchcraft as a collection of eccentric, old ladies with black hats and a fetish for cats (dead or alive); and riding brooms, whilst turning children who make messes in their rooms into frogs. However, people in Africa or for that matter, many other nations around the world; perceive 'witchcraft' as a very fearsome power that can potentially cause great good or horrible evil, depending on the person using this demonically driven power and their motives behind such an action.

Now beloved, to truly understand what I'm talking about, it's important to clearly identify witchcraft in its' most basic form. Because once we can identify this spirit and its' capabilities, then we will begin to see more clearly what is happening in the spirit realm; and also, then we will be able to rid ourselves from the terrible oppression, this spirit causes, when unleashed upon ourselves or indeed upon others who have opened the door for such a spirit to torment them.

Witchcraft is basically rooted in the fear of man, and "the fear of man is a snare" for most certainly, when we begin to fear people or circumstances more than we fear God; then we fall victim to the spirit of witchcraft; and it will attach itself to our minds which are in the soul realm. Beloved, the root of 'witchcraft' is the use of wrongful authority or counterfeit spiritual authority to cause us to fall victim to its' power.

To better understand this phenomenon, let me give you a word picture that you'll never forget; and perhaps this word picture will enable you to take in the seriousness of this spiritual attack.

Here, before you is an African village. There are 50 people including women and children, and there is a Chief of the village, and there is also a witch doctor. The Chief is the chief by bloodline, or he achieved his rank in battle; and he exercises his authority as chiefs do.

The witch doctor may continue on through many chiefs' reigns and is usually hidden away in some back corner of the African village, doing what he does best. This can include the art or practice of preparing substances, whether vegetable, mineral or animal, for the purposes of medicine or pharmacy, and the preparation of drugs. Thus, the evidence of drug abuse, such as smoking, or drinking can help to identify a spirit of witchcraft in operation.

Here are some questions which may help us identify the existence of this type pf spiritual attack upon our lives:

1. Who is the rightful authority in the village?
2. Who actually runs the village?
3. How does he run the village without authority?

Answers:
1. The rightful authority in the village is the chief.
2. The one who runs the village is the witch doctor.
3. He controls the Chief and the village by fear by three main tactics.

**Manipulation ... Intimidation ... Domination**

So, you may ask: 'Should the Chief, as the rightful authority, make a move to do something, which is against what the witch doctor would not personally like or does not fit into the witch doctor's personal agenda?' This is extremely unwise, for the Witch Doctor would let the Chief know in one of these three ways, His objection to the Chief's intentions. This is exactly how the Spirit of Witchcraft works beloved, through 'Manipulation, Intimidation, and then Total Domination.'

The Witch Doctor could show his objections to the Chief by "pointing a bone or a curse" at him. However normally, the Chief (or indeed his father before him), would have already been manipulated, intimidated and indeed dominated, The sad truth is, the Chief is being held captive by the Witch Doctor, as he submits to the power of spiritual witchcraft which works through the Witch Doctor by inflicting fear and intimidation, hence, controlling the Chief to such an extent, that he influences any decisions that are made. And so in effect, there is wrongful authority over both him and his village. And beloved, the existence of this witchcraft can only persist, if the subject of the witchcraft spirit allows it to remain, either by fear or ignorance.

Witchcraft or manipulation is normally based upon deception and half-truths; as it is usually harder to manipulate people with the absolute truth,' but not impossible. An example of the latter would be 'blackmail,' which is in general, an evil work of man or 'the flesh,' and is very opposed to God's laws. Intimidation is the act of making people fearful, or the state of being abashed or confused with shame, confounded, and put to silence. Witchcraft influenced domination, is an exercise of power and it is truly an arbitrary authority, which exacts tyranny in every exercise of power, it wields. A good example of this type of domination would be the Nazi regime during World War II.

Another simple example is: when we try to use emotional pressure to manipulate others. Beloved, such basic forms of inducement can open us up for a spirit of witchcraft, and if such behaviour becomes a pattern, it can become abusive towards others. An additional example is, when businessmen scheme to find pressure points while pursuing a deal. This too can be a form of witchcraft; if it works to influence others in such a way, that it is not in the client's best interests. Beloved, many of the manipulative methods promoted as sales tactics in marketing today; are indeed basic forms of manipulation, and can certainly go terribly wrong, as a spirit of witchcraft enters in and corrupts the salesmen's' motives and actions.

Another example may be, a young child throwing a tantrum in public, or in everyday family life. Beloved, it the child remains uncorrected, then that same child may grow up and learn to control his/her parents by displaying bad behaviour; and then later on, control their spouses by way of withdrawing affection or sulking. Thus, achieving total domination of all his or her family members, by only displaying good behaviour when he or she gets their own way; in any given situation. Sadly, as the manipulation and witchcraft spirits increase their dominion in these circumstances, often paranoia in the people being held captive sets in, and they may then blame themselves for the person's very bad behaviour, which is motivated by these spirits. Such spirits will then have such a stronghold within the family; that they will then become irrationally consumed with driving out or destroying anyone who threatens their control over the relationships within that family.

Charismatic Witchcraft is a form of manipulation, which is seldom known these days as black magic, but rather as a form of "white witchcraft." This includes well-meaning people who do not have the confidence to be straightforward and have therefore fallen into subtle forms of manipulation to gain influence.

The source of witchcraft against us may not be the obvious satanic cults or New Age operatives. But by far, the worst offenders are Christians, (though deceived); who are in fact, praying against us, instead of for us. An example of this would be a 'directive prayer'. This is where Christians may take authority "Where they have none" over someone else's lives and pray (for example): "Lord change his heart or change his mind". I would ask then: "What authority do they have to require such a thing?" While admittedly, they most certainly have the authority to pray: "Change my heart or my own mind" yet when it comes to another, it's unlikely these Christians have true authority to pray in such a way. It is much better to pray "blessings over them and that God's perfect will, would abound in their lives."

Beloved, the reasons that such prayers have such power is, because God's word says in Matthew 18:18: "Whatever is released on earth is released in heaven, and whatever is bound on earth is bound in heaven." And truly, if intercession is motivated by a spirit of control or manipulation, then this opens up the door for the operation of the spirit of witchcraft; and Satan can then use these types of prayers to cause hindrances for the person being prayed for.

In fact, such prayers or incantations performed by witch doctors in Africa, have been known to cause grave illness and even death. Beloved, the Spirit of Witchcraft is demonic, and yet, if we are committed Christians then the Holy Spirit protects us from such dire consequences.

Nevertheless, if we fail to recognise such oppression brought on by wrongful prayers, then we may experience harassment and hindrances that we neither need nor want. Once however; we identify the Spirit of Witchcraft is at work in our circumstances, we then have full authority in the name of Jesus to command the thing to go; but we must adjust our behaviour; so that we do not provide open doors for the Spirit of Witchcraft to attack us in future or ever again.

Beloved, remember the Spirit of Witchcraft can cause discouragement, confusion, depression, loss of vision, disorientation, withdrawal and defeat.

Here is a description of the types of sin conditions or strongholds which may result if such a spirit causes oppression in a person's life.

## DISCOURAGEMENT

Everyone gets discouraged at times, and it can be for many different reasons, so this is not always the result of witchcraft being used against us. But, if we become subject to increasing discouragement for no apparent reason, witchcraft should be considered a possible source. When everything seems to go wrong, and the difficulties begin to seem insurmountable, then you are probably coming under spiritual attack. The main strategy for afflicting you with discouragement is to weaken you for the next level of attack, which is usually:

## CONFUSION

Again, we must look for a general and increasing "spirit of confusion" for which there is no apparent reason. Here we begin to lose our clarity; as to just what we have been called to do, which of course will weaken our resolve. This confusion is meant to compound the discouragement, making us even weaker and more vulnerable to further attack, which will usually come in the form of:

## DEPRESSION

This is a deeper problem than simple discouragement; it is an unshakeable dread that is the result of both discouragement and confusion combined, along with a general negligence in spiritual disciplines that has usually slipped away by this time.

## LOSS OF VISION

This is the goal of the previous demonic attacks and works to increase the effect of all of them. Here we begin to doubt our calling altogether. And the only way that we can sail through the storm of confusion is to hold our course. And beloved, we cannot hold our course, if we do not know where we are going. We will not try to hold our course, if we begin to think it was wrong for us to go in the first place. This will lead to our drifting in circles at the time when we most need to "make straight paths for our feet." This sets us up for the next level of assault:

## DISORIENTATION

This is the combined result of depression, confusion and loss of vision. At this level we have not just forgotten the course we are supposed to be holding onto, but we have even lost our ability to read the compass. The Scriptures will no longer speak to us, and we will not trust the Lord's voice. This is the point of spiritual incapacitation, the inability to function, which results in:

## WITHDRAWAL

This comes when we begin to withdraw or retreat from our purpose in the ministry and often from our families and others we are close to. Withdrawal will result in DESPAIR.

## DESPAIR

Withdrawal from the battle leads quickly to hopelessness and without hope; we can easily be taken out, either through temptation, sickness or death. Even science has proven that when hope is removed, often the healthiest person will quickly deteriorate and die. With hope, men and women have lived long past the point when a normal body would have quit. DESPAIR will always lead to DEFEAT.

It is through these things, that witchcraft not only controls, but destroys relationships and people. Therefore, it is very important that we refuse to take authority over things or people or places that are not ours. And we should absolutely humble ourselves and wait for God to open doors for us; without striving in our own power and strength. Beloved, any authority or influence that we gain by our own manipulation or self,- promotion; will be a stumbling block to us, and might even result in the downfall of others, for the Bible says "Pride goes before a fall" in (Proverbs 16:18).

A very powerful Bible verse that we can use successfully to rid ourselves of demonic oppression is in (Mark 3: 27): "In fact, no one can enter a strong man's house without first tying him up." "Then he can plunder the strong man's house."

So beloved, you may ask what is a strong man? A strong man is a spirit power in the Heavens. It is important to remember when the Bible speaks about the heavens; it is referring to the spiritual or supernatural realm. Spirit powers can often be Jezebel, Anti-Christ, or Death & Hell spirits. A Strongman is different from a principality, who has dominion over a specific location, or has a designated target area. However, the principality may have characteristics of spirit powers such as: Jezebel, Anti-Christ, or Death & Hell. Their existence is substantiated in the Bible through Ephesians 6:12, which says: "For our wrestling is not against flesh and blood, but against the rulers, against the powers, against the world's rulers of this darkness, and against the spiritual forces of wickedness in the heavenly places;"

And so, in referring to (Mark 3:27): you might also ask, what exactly is his house? (1 Corinthians 3:16), says: "Don't you know that you yourselves are God's temple (house), and that God's Spirit dwells in your midst?

The Spirit of Jezebel which is also a well-known witchcraft spirit; is mentioned in the bible and without question, is the nastiest, evil, most disgusting, cunning, and seductive spirit in Satan's hierarchy. This evil spirit has been responsible for not only tearing down churches, pastors, and different Christian ministries; but it has also been responsible for breaking up many marriages, friendships, companies, along with getting many people to commit cold-blooded murders and suicides.

For those of you who have been oppressed by this evil spirit, or have encountered it in some form, you will know exactly how much damage it can cause, as it wreaks havoc in people's lives. The Jezebel Spirit is without question, one of the most evil and vile things I personally, have ever come across in my life; and like Satan, its' master, this type of spirit is simply pure evil. Over the last 20 years or so, I have encountered this spirit myself numerous times, with it usually being attached to a specific person each time I have encountered it. And with this being the case, I would like to discuss in this chapter, what a Jezebel spirit is, and how you can identify it, should you be challenged with such a witchcraft spirit in the future.

The Jezebel Spirit is a "type" of evil spirit in Satan's kingdom. There is only one devil, one Satan, but there are many spirits that would be considered a Jezebel type spirit, as they all have a particular type of personality, and a specific way in which they like to operate. The reason why many deliverance ministers have used the term, "Jezebel spirit," is because of the nature of its' personality and the way it operates once it sets up shop within someone. The word "Jezebel" originates from the Old Testament story of Queen Jezebel during the days of Elijah, the prophet. She was a ruling queen at that time, and she had cold-bloodedly killed many of God's prophets during her reign. As mentioned in 1 Kings Chapter 19.

The Identifiable Characteristics of the Jezebel Spirit are as follows:

1. While it's almost unrecognizable at first, such individuals are threatened by a prophetic leader, who is the main target of concern. Although such people will seem to have prophetic gifts, their aim is to actually control those who move in the prophetic realm.
2. To increase their favour, such individuals often zero in on a pastor or a leader in business, or perhaps close staff members and then seek to find the weakest link in order to subdue them. Their eventual goal is to run the church or business.
3. Seeking to gain popular and pastoral or business leader endorsement, such individuals will form strategic affiliations with people who are perceived by others to be spiritual or influential with others.
4. To appear spiritual, or of some level of importance; such individuals will seek recognition by manipulating situations to gain an advantage. Such individuals often conjure up dreams and visions from their imaginations, or inspired ideas they borrow from others.
5. When these individuals receive initial recognition, they often respond with false humility. However, this trait is short-lived.
6. When confronted, these individuals will become defensive. They will justify their actions with phrases like, "I'm just

following God" or "God told me to do this." Or "I am just keen to get up the career ladder, as quickly as possible."
7. These individuals will often allege having great spiritual or business insight into church government and business affairs, but they will not appeal to proper authority. Rather they first appeal to others. Often their opinion becomes the "last word" on matters, thereby elevating their thoughts above the pastor's or business leaders.'
8. Having impure motives, these individuals will seek out others, desiring to have "disciples," needing constant affirmation from their followers.
9. Desiring to avoid accountability, these individuals prefer to pray for people in isolated situations—in a corner or in another room. Thus, innuendos and false "prophetic" words cannot be easily challenged. Or in a place of business, they may look for shortcuts to make it look like they are more efficient then they truly are.
10. Eager to gain control, these people will gather others and seek to teach them. While the teachings may begin correctly, "doctrine" is often established that is not supported by the Word of God. In a business atmosphere, the person may sabotage other potential business colleagues in order to ensure they stay in the limelight at all times.
11. Deceiving others by soulish prophecy or by giving words that someone wants to hear, these individuals seek to gain credibility. They prophesy half-truths or little known facts, as though they were from God. Such individuals may also take advantage of someone else's poor memory by twisting their previous prophecies to make it seem as if their words have come to pass. In business, the person may speak in

half-truths to twist situations, so they work in his or her favour.

12. Although the "laying on of hands" is biblical, these individuals like to impart a higher level in the spirit—or break down walls that have held someone back—by the "laying on of hands." However, their touch is actually a curse. Instead of a holy blessing, an evil spirit may be imparted. In business, the person may develop a fault-finding attitude and cause a loss of morale amongst the staff he or she works with.

13. Masking poor self-esteem with spiritual pride, these individuals want to be seen as the most spiritual ones in the church. They may be the first to cry, wail, or mourn—claiming a burden from God. However, they are no different from the Pharisees, who announced their gifts in order to be seen by men. In business, the person may strive in her or she's own strength for recognition and accomplishment and when he or she is unable to reach that goal the blame game is often utilized in ensuring others are blamed for any failures.

14. Usually, such individual's family lives are shaky. These individuals may be single or married. If married, their spouse is usually weak spiritually, unsaved, or just apathetic. They begin to dominate and control everyone in the family.

The ruling spirit under Jezebel is DECEPTION; which encompasses the following sin conditions and spiritual strongholds:

Addictions, adultery, arrogance, broken marriages, charms, divination, drugs, fear, feminism, filthiness (of the spirit & flesh), fornication, free love, hatred, harlotry, heresies, homosexuality, idolatry, incest & indecency (this usually comes as a result of a curse from a previous generation involved in idolatry), jealousy, lasciviousness, lust, unclean thoughts, masturbation, occultist things, perverted sexual acts, oral sex, false religions (such as: Mormonism, and Jehovah's witnesses), pride, sorcery, Spiritism, spiritual blindness (such as: freemasonry, Mormonism), spirit of religion, witchcraft, i.e. domination, manipulation, intimidation, lying, blasphemy, covetousness, and embracing humanism, new age mindsets.

The Antichrist Spirit is mentioned several times in God's Word and is another powerful spiritual power that oppresses mankind in a ruthless and cruel manner. (I John 2:18), talks about this spirit and says: "Little children, it is the end times: and as ye have heard, the antichrist shall come, and even now are there many antichrists; whereby we know that it is the last time; also,. (2 Thessalonians 2: 3-4), says: "Let no man deceive you by any means: for that day shall not come, except there comes a falling away first, and that a man of sin be revealed, the son of perdition; who opposeth and exalteth himself above all that is called Godly, or that is worshipped; so that he as God sitteth in the temple of God, shewing himself that he is God."

Beloved, without a doubt the predominant sin of the Spirit of Antichrist is Pride, the other sin conditions and strongholds resulting from this ruling spirit are as follows: Spirits of anger, bitterness, blasphemy, corrupt communications, curses, dissension, drunkenness, envy or hatred, filthy language, lack of faith, lying, malice, murder, nightmares, outbursts of wrath, poverty, rebellion, spirit of wretchedness, rejection, selfish ambitions, stealing, strife, torment, unbelief, Unforgiveness, lawlessness, and contention.

The Third prevailing ruling spirit which causes spiritual oppression is the Spirit of Death and Hell: In Revelations 6:8 it describes this spirit power by saying: "I looked, and there before me was a pale horse! Its' rider was named Death, and Hades was following close behind him. They were given power over a fourth of the earth to kill by sword, famine and plague, and by the wild beasts of the earth."

This spirit causes the following, mishaps, sin conditions, and strongholds:

Frequent accidents, succession of deaths in families; sickness, disease, pain, plagues on Christians, breathing problems, miscarriages, boils, barrenness, guilt, condemnation, decay & corruption, mildew & mustiness, famine & pestilence (of land & spirit) prayers blocked, discouragement, confusion, depression, loss of vision, disorientation, withdrawal, despair, (In short others will prosper but everything you do will fail).

Beloved, as mentioned before, we have complete authority given to us by Jesus Christ, when He died upon the cross and made the supreme sacrifice to save us from sin, sickness, sorrow, and death. But we must first walk before God as holy and committed Christians, to ensure we are not opening doors to Satan and these demonic spirits. And secondly, if we have already opened the door to demonic oppression through our disobedience; then we must repent, and then take authority in the name of Jesus Christ and the Power of the Holy Spirit to gain complete victory and close the door forever over these terrible and oppressive spirits. Amen!

# Chapter 16

## A Deeper Understanding of Joy and Why it Strengthens Us

Having grown up with a Christian mother, I have heard most of my life the scripture verse: "The joy of the Lord is my strength," from (Nehemiah 8:10); and to be honest, I found the scripture rather annoying, at times; because I couldn't see how anyone could feel joy or have any degree of humour, when they or indeed I, faced such horrendous struggles in life. Because when I was a young Christian, I still strived for many things in my own strength; rather than going to God, the Father; for guidance and breakthrough. And as a result, I became disheartened, confused, and disillusioned a lot of the time, and opened up the door for demonic oppression to afflict me with discouragement and hopelessness for over a year. And because of my disobedience, I suffered in that state much longer than I should have done, until I finally rose up and took authority over those strongholds in the name of Jesus and received my breakthrough.

The truth is beloved, Satan is not very original with His methods of oppressing us, and if he afflicted us once with a strategy that was somewhat successful; then as time passes He will most assuredly try to use the same tactics again to attack your body or soul, when you are in a vulnerable state at any given time in your life.

Beloved, I can certainly confirm that this did happen to me in my own life, when I was a mature Christian, and had been a minister of the gospel for over 15 years. At the time, my husband was very ill in the hospital and had an ongoing chronic condition which caused such a change in his personality and behaviour; that he was not the same person that I had married, and I had great despair and hopelessness concerning his condition. In fact, I was so battered with demonic oppression, I felt like I, myself was falling into the same pit that my husband had fallen into; and that I would never find my way out of it, and I could barely make it through from one day to the next.

Beloved believe me, I did not walk around with joy and singing during those terrible, dark days. But I can say that in spite of my deep despair and hopelessness and my disobedience in not turning to Him; that God still loved me and understood my pain, and even though I stayed in that oppressed state for nearly a year, I did have the assurance deep down in my heart that God had not forsaken me. I also knew that I could turn to Him and He would take all of my burdens from me at any time, if I chose to give them to Him. So why you might ask, when I was an experienced minister of the gospel, did I not just turn my burdens over to God immediately? Well, the truth is beloved; I listened to the demons who were whispering in my ear saying: "You have been a faithful servant of God and look what has happened to your life." You see beloved, during that time; we had to give up ministry entirely and all of our so called Christian friends had abandoned us, because of the nature and ugliness of my husband's chronic condition; and I became very bitter against God, that He had allowed such a thing to come upon us. God's word says in (Proverbs 14:10): "The heart knows its own bitterness and no stranger shares its' joy." And this scripture was certainly true in my case, as I felt so totally and completely alone, as former friends and even family members alienated me time and time again. Until one day, I remembered the joy I had once felt whilst I was in fellowship with the Lord; and I cried before the Lord and repented of my bitterness and anger towards Him. I then asked God, my Father, to take me back into His fold and envelope me with His wonderful joy and grace. And from that very moment, beloved, God, the Father gave me such a beautiful impartation of His presence (through the Holy Spirit) during my prayer time; that my hopelessness and despair were immediately swept away, and His great joy was deposited securely into my heart and remains gloriously there to this day.

This beloved, I believe is the true 'Joy of the Lord.' For just the innate knowing that we have, God, the Father, and He is there, loving us and ready and willing to help us through the good times and the bad, as we walk through the journey of life, is a very precious thing. I believe His loving ways towards us are depicted in this wonderful scripture, Isaiah 40:31, which says: "But those who hope in the LORD will renew their strength. They will soar on wings like eagles; they will run and not grow weary; they will walk and not be faint." God further declares His great love for us, by saying in (Jeremiah 31:3): "I have loved you with an everlasting love; I have drawn you with unfailing kindness." He even has assigned angels to watch over us beloved, lest we dash our feet and fall, as is confirmed in the Bible in Psalm 91:11: "For he will command his angels concerning you to guard you in all your ways;" and in (Luke

4:10-11): For it is written: "'He will command his angels concerning you, to guard you carefully; they will lift you up in their hands, so that you will not strike your foot against a stone" Beloved, a Godly inspired joy is essential for your health and wellbeing, scientists have even proven the important link between joy and good health which substantiates this Godly principle; which is spoken about in Proverbs 17:22: "A joyful heart is good medicine, but a crushed spirit dries up the bones."

In fact, Ruut Veenhoven, a Dutch researcher, carefully reviewed and analysed 30 separate studies on the relationship between joy and health. And Veenhoven concluded from his studies, "that joyful people are less likely to fall sick," "and joy," he discovered, "actually adds more years to a person's life." Coincidentally, numerous other health studies have proven that joy boosts the immune system, lowers stress hormones, decreases pain, and relaxes the muscles and prevents heart disease.

Beloved, the human system, in its' fallen state, is certain to regress under the stress and strain of life. Our physical frame simply cannot hold up, if our mental, emotional and spiritual states of being are dampened. And nothing strengthens our emotions and mental state like the spiritual force of joy. The joy of the Lord is not some passing emotion that is dependent on the availability of the fine material things of life. But instead, the joy of the Lord is a boundless energy provided by the Holy Spirit which flows through our human spirits and wells up into an eternal gladness. Beloved, I have experienced this joy which is the wellspring of life, and I can confirm that this life force gives strength to every part of our beings and keeps us in sound health. The same Spirit that raised Jesus Christ from the dead is in us and quickens our mortal bodies by touching us with the powerful glory of God. So beloved, we have a spiritual force of joy that sadly this world knows nothing about, but we can share if we choose to, and this is our strength and continual source of good health.

A cheerful spirit and gladness of heart produces tremendous health effects; and we can trust the joy of the Lord to sustain our health, just as we can trust it to give us strength and raise us up from sickness. The Bible records that the Lord gave the Israelites great joy after they had made a commitment to obedience and adherence to the Word of God. We can likewise activate and preserve the joy of the Lord by ensuring that we have an attitude of continuous praise and singing and also, by studying and adhering to the Word of God. This will bring health to our flesh and life to our bones. And sickness or demonic oppression simply cannot have any power or dominion over us, because the joy of the Lord is our strength, in the name of Jesus, Christ, our Lord. Hallelujah!

# Chapter 17

## The Necessity of Fellowship with the Holy Spirit

Beloved, Jesus said to His disciples that He had to leave, so the Comforter could come, as is written in (John 16:7); "But very truly I tell you, it is for your good that I am going away. Unless I go away, the Comforter will not come to you; but if I go, I will send Him to you." And the Comforter is the Holy Spirit; and this powerful force is our very access to God; as we walk each day in the purpose and destiny, God has given us. Jesus also said in (John 14:16): "And I will pray to the Father, and He shall give you another Comforter, that He may abide with you forever;" Beloved, Jesus said that God, the Father was giving us another Comforter, which is the Holy Spirit that was like Him (for the Holy Spirit is part of the Godhead which God, the Father, Jesus His Son, and the Holy Spirit, are one) And the Holy Spirit ,who works as a Holy Person of the Godhead; leads, guides, and empowers us always, just like Jesus did with His disciples, Hallelujah!. This is a powerful truth, beloved, that can absolutely change your life once you fully understand the true depth of what God is offering us.

Every living creature wants fellowship; and we feel sad when we get lonely; and if we do not know how to fellowship with the Holy Spirit, sometimes we will seek to fill the gap with things or people that will never, ever satisfy us. Many of us want relationship with God; but we don't know how to really fellowship with the Holy Spirit? In fact, multitudes of believers never actually develop a relationship with the very one who dwells inside of them. Let me reiterate beloved, that all Christians get a measure of the Holy Spirit when they are saved; but there is a larger impartation of the Holy Spirit which can also be accessed, as is stated in (1 Corinthians 12:3): "Therefore I want you to know that no one who is speaking by the Spirit of God says, "Jesus be cursed," and no one can say, "Jesus is Lord," except by the Holy Spirit; and in (Mark 1:8), which says: "I baptise you with water; but He will baptise you with the Holy Spirit." Beloved most human beings want fellowship, and they often feel empty and broken, when they are alone. And if we are committed Christians, then we all want relationship with God. But how many of us, really know how to fellowship with the Holy Spirit? Well, the sad truth is, that although multitudes of Christians believe in God, they never actually develop a relationship with the very one, who dwells inside of them. And as a result, many of us feel like orphans all alone with no Father, and no one to help guide us through life; because of this lack of knowledge.

Beloved, the Holy Spirit wants our friendship! We are His temple and He knows everything about everything, as is written in, (I Corinthians 3:16-20): "Do you not know that you are a temple of God and that the Spirit of God dwells in you? If any man destroys the temple of God, God will destroy him, for the temple of God is holy, and that is what you are. Let no man deceive himself. If any man among you thinks that he is wise in this age, he must become foolish, so that he may become wise. For the wisdom of this world is foolishness before God.

For it is written, "He is The One Who catches the wise in their craftiness; and again, The Lord knows the reasonings of the wise, and that they are useless."

Beloved, God wants to reveal through the Holy Spirit the deep things of His kingdom to us, as is confirmed in (1 Corinthians 2:9). "However, as it is written: 'What no eye has seen, what no ear has heard, and what no human mind has conceived' -- the things God has prepared for those who love Him." The Holy Spirit has been sent to give us God's power, revelation and strength, and we can fellowship with Him for He is God living in us."

An anecdote I recently read, explains this need very well and perhaps this story will help you to understand the necessity of fellowshipping with the Holy Spirit more clearly. "A lady went to a jeweller to get her watch fixed. He disappeared and came back quickly with her watch running perfectly. She asked him, *"How could you fix it in such a short time?"* And He told her that it only needed a small battery. And all the time, the lady had been trying to wind the watch; and she never knew that she only needed a battery to keep it running perfectly."

Beloved, this story describes a women that is so much like us, as we live a Christian life, Because, many times we do not realize the inner power that we have in the Holy Spirit; and how He can run everything in our life so perfectly; if we will only learn to listen to His still small voice, But so very often, we think we must take matters into our own hands, and we reason with our own minds and strive to find favour and success in our lives, and we end up leaving God totally out of any decisions we make, altogether. And so, we live powerless lives, and even though we may achieve some measure of success, we end up feeling empty and alone, as we face the many challenges and pressures that may result from such achievements. Or, if failures result from our striving without God, then we face unimaginable demonic oppression and torment, as the enemy seeks to destroy us so completely, that any relationship we once had with God, is just a distant memory.

Beloved, a lack of reality, godliness, power, and fruit in our lives is due to unbelief and our lack of fellowship with the Holy Spirit. We need to go deeper in partnership with the Holy Spirit; if we want to live powerful lives. The truth is many of us are living life with a dead battery. We feel dead inside. We must begin fellowshipping with the Holy Spirit; and He will bring new life and empowerment to our spirits and lives! And He will show us the way to find purpose and fulfilment in every area or our lives.

Fellowship with the Holy Spirit is not complicated. It's all about a two-way dialogue. We must learn to share our hearts freely with the Holy Spirit; by just starting a conversation with Him, and He will speak back to us. But we must stay engaged. He wants our heart connection. Out of our abiding connection with Him, the Holy Spirit will flow and all issues that concern us in our lives, can be taken care of entirely, as we turn our burdens over to Him. (Proverbs 4:23) says: "Guard your heart above all else, for it determines the course of your life." Beloved, your heart is the spirit within you that God longs to commune with through the person of the Holy Spirit.

You might ask, well how do I know that it is God that is speaking to me? And I can only tell you from my own experience, that it is indeed a still small voice that you will hear, (to me it sounds like someone on a long distance telephone call); and that voice will most assuredly line up with God's character and likeness which is described in: (1 Corinthians 13: 4-8): "Love is patient, love in is kind. It does not envy, it does not boast, it is not proud. It does not dishonour others, it is not self-seeking, it is not easily angered, it keeps no record of wrongs. Love does not delight in evil but rejoices with the truth. It always protects, always trusts, always hopes, always perseveres.

Now beloved, I will not say that God has never given me Words, that have seemed quite stern towards others; but I know that since God "does not delight in evil and rejoices in truth," that at times His direction through the Holy Spirit may require faith, as I have sought to walk in obedience to fulfil His purposes. In fact, I remember a Word I once had from the Holy Spirit, of which He impressed upon me, to give to a fellow Pastor many years ago. This direction from the Holy Spirit was very hard for me; because this fellow pastor was a respected minister within the network I belonged to, and yet, the Holy Spirit impressed upon me 'day and night' to deliver the prophetic word to that man. Finally, I went to the fellow pastor's church office (feeling literally sick in my body), and I delivered the prophetic word, just as the Lord had spoken to me, which was: "for him to stop allowing a false prophet to speak in his church or judgement would fall upon him for his disobedience." Now Beloved, I don't mind telling you this seemed a very harsh word to me; but then I cannot deny that God speaks quite boldly in His Word about how he hates witchcraft and false prophets, who walk under the influence of demonic power, as is spoken about in (Jeremiah 14:14): "Then the LORD said to me, The prophets prophesy lies in my name: I sent them not, neither have I commanded them, neither spoken to them: they prophesy to you a false vision and divination, and a thing of nothing, and the deceit of their heart."

A false vision and divination given to individuals in a church by false prophets is a very devastating thing, which can effectively destroy a church entirely, for it can divide and conquer God's work from within, as Satan literally attaches a witchcraft spirit to the people's souls and can cause them to believe in a lie. Beloved, the definition of divination is: "the art or practice that seeks to foresee or foretell future events or discover hidden knowledge usually by the interpretation of omens or by the aid of supernatural powers," which in the case of false prophets would be from the demonic powers of witchcraft. Sadly, the Pastor laughed at me, and did not listen to the prophetic word God gave me at the time; and in the years following, his wife committed suicide, and his son resorted to a life of crime, rejecting God entirely. The church itself has suffered people dying prematurely at a young age, and its' people have been afflicted with an inordinate amount of cancer and other types of terrible illnesses. But it still stands and prospers, due to the heart of faithful intercessors in the church who have sought after God's compassion and love, despite Satan's master plan. Hallelujah!

Beloved, it is important to learn to linger in presence of the Holy Spirit without rushing Him; and speak affectionately, slowly, softly, and briefly with short phrases to Him. Pause and listen to His still, small voice. And then, journal your thoughts and what you believe He is saying to you. And your confidence will then build as you learn to hear His voice more and more.

One way to enhance your fellowship with the Holy Spirit (which I believe is very helpful), is to use these five practical phrases by using the acrostic **T-R-U-S-T**.

- T - Thank you -Thank the Holy Spirit for His indwelling presence. And approach God through thanksgiving (Psalm 100:1-5). Pray, *"Thank you Holy Spirit for your presence in me, for your guidance, etc. I love your leadership..."*

- R - Release revelation - Ask the Holy Spirit to reveal to you His heart and open your eyes to the realm of His glory. (Ephesians 1:17-19) is a great prayer and pray, *"Holy Spirit, open my eyes to see the realm of God's glory. Open the eyes of my understanding, give me the spirit of wisdom and understanding."*

- U - Use me - Ask the Holy Spirit to use you more and more. Put your desire to be used before Him and expect Him to use you every day. Pray, *"Thank you Holy Spirit for releasing your power and gifts through my life. Use me fully for your glory..."*

- S - Strengthen me - Ask the Holy Spirit to strengthen your mind, will, and emotions with His divine might, so that you may contain more of His wisdom, fruit, and gifts. See (Ephesians 3:16). Pray, *"Thank you Holy Spirit for your love, patience, joy, etc. Increase my capacity to contain more of your wisdom, gifts, and fruit..."*

- T - Teach me - Ask the Holy Spirit to teach you about God's Word and ways. Ask Him to manifest His leadership in every area of your life. He will order your steps and give you new and creative ideas. See (John 14:26 and 16:13). Pray, *"Holy Spirit let me see what you see and feel what you feel. Release it with power through my life..."*

I remember as a young girl visiting a place called Hoover Dam, which is located outside of Boulder City, Nevada, in the United States, and how the sheer power of the dam impressed me, as the tour director explained: "How the dam worked powerfully from within the mountain, as the great turbines and generators transformed the power of tons and tons of water into electricity." And all of this was happening quietly and without notice deep within a huge mountain of rock and earth.

Beloved, in the same way, it is the Holy Spirit who is working deeply within each of our lives. He gives us the power to walk in God's victory and grace, as we are guided by His voice. And His deep work in our lives, gives us power and makes us like a river of living water, able to touch others with His mighty power, which is known as God's anointing. This is spoken about in (John 7:37-39), which says: "On the last and greatest day of the festival, Jesus stood and said in a loud voice, "Let anyone who is thirsty come to me and drink. Whoever believes in me, as scripture has said, rivers of living water will flow from within them."

Beloved, by this, Jesus meant the Spirit, of whom those who believed in Him were later to receive. Up to that time, the Spirit had not been given, since Jesus had not yet been glorified.

The anointing of the Holy Spirit gives us the power to not only break off strongholds in our own life; but also to do so in the lives of others as we carry out God's will and extend His love and grace to an oppressed and dying world. This is spoken about in (1 John 2:27), which says: "As for you, the anointing you received from Him remains in you, and you do not need anyone to teach you. But as His anointing teaches you about all things and as that anointing is real, not counterfeit--just as it has taught you, remain in Him."

Just as His true and genuine anointing teaches you about all things; so, you can remain in Him," so that you can grow in confidence of His leading, as you fellowship with Him on a daily basis. There are certainly anointed men and women of God, who have knowledge that the Holy Spirit has imparted to them also, that you can learn or gain direction from. But beloved, I firmly believe that this scripture is meant to encourage you to listen to the Holy Spirit, for yourself, so that you can gain power and direction for your own life, as He imparts and speaks wisdom and truth to you, so you can walk in His ways for a glorious future, Amen!

# Chapter 18

## The Life-Giving Power of Praise and Worship

Beloved, it never ceases to amaze me, how the Holy Spirit can move so powerfully through the open doors provided by our praise and worship of the Almighty God. We are sensitive creatures by nature and the purity of this form of worship, can pierce the very core of our beings and can open us up to God's lifesaving and healing grace like nothing else can. There is literally an atmospheric change in the supernatural realm that occurs; as the sweet praise and worship of God's people rises like sweet smelling incense unto our Creator. And the power of such sweet praises is swiftly made evident, as God grants His healing rain of salvation, favour and breakthrough upon human hearts in an otherwise dry and desolate land.

During my life as a Christian minister, I have seen great miracles happen as a direct result of praise and worship. For this mighty connection created between people and the Living God through praise, has in fact, enabled these same hurting people to embrace God's healing and lifesaving power, as the anointing causes their faith to rise to receive from the Lord. This occurs, because all barriers have been torn down by the Spirit of God, which has been released through His people praising Him. One such day comes to mind, when we were praising God in a church I pastored in Jasper, Texas, many years ago. That sunny day, I was leading worship and the power of God was so heavy in the service, that I could hardly stand upright. Now for those of you who don't know where Jasper, Texas is, it is a small town located in the beautiful lake and forestlands of East Texas. And on that particular Sunday morning, we were praising the Lord with all of our hearts; and about midway through our praise service, two families, (who I later found out had been camping near one of the lakes, that weekend), came into our midst and joined in with our praise and worship to the Lord.

Now this family looked like the "walking wounded" to me, as two of them had casts on their legs and one had a terrible rash, and there was one person with her arm in a sling. But we just kept right on singing and praising the Lord, as God's Presence was heavy upon us and we could do little else. About ten minutes passed by as we soaked in the Presence of the Lord, and suddenly I heard what sounded like a great shout of joy; and I saw one man in the group throw His crutch against the wall and then he stood up and walked boldly to the front, and said loudly with a big grin on his face: "I am healed, God has healed me." I patted the man on the back and said in agreement with Him: "Praise God, God is good," and the anointing of His power was so great in the place, tears were literally streaming down my face with joy.

And that small East Texas congregation went wild with excitement and gave thanks to God, as they clapped and cheered, praising God, and the music and praise unto God never stopped. It wasn't long before the woman with the sling on her arm, also ran to the front where I was standing and literally screamed out in excitement: "Look at my arm, it is no longer sprained, God has healed it!" And she was flexing her arm up and down rapidly to demonstrate God's mighty, healing power. I began swaying under the power of God and said with heartfelt thanks over the microphone; "Thank you God for your wonderful healing grace in touching these people today," but I did not feel in my Sprit that God was done yet; and continued to lead worship and was mightily blessed; as I then saw the first man who had been healed, cut his cast off with a pen knife, and then start to dance before the Lord.

And then no more than five minutes went by, and I heard a third shout from the vicinity of the visitors, saying "Lord I believe in You," and the other person with the cast, a middle-aged woman, limped up with her teenage daughter, who had a terrible blotchy, red rash over her face, shoulders, and arms, and they approached the front where I stood, and the woman said: "Please pray for us, I believe God wants to heal me and my daughter today." Humbled, by her faith, I did not hesitate and before I began to pray, I motioned to the worship team behind me to keep playing, and then reached over to touch her and begin to pray; but before I could even utter a word out of my mouth, I felt the Holy Spirit move through my arm and then both the mother and daughter fell upon the floor; completely under the healing power of God, Praise the Lord!

Now Beloved, only a few moments passed by and I can gloriously report that both mother and daughter were miraculously healed. The mother who had a torn ligament in her foot due to a boating accident, could not only walk when she got up off the floor; but she ran around the main hall of our church; and there was not a blotch to be seen on her lovely teenage daughter, Hallelujah!

It is my firm belief that this powerful praise and worship of the Almighty God, Jehovah, actually breaks down the barriers between ourselves and God in such a way, that all oppressing spirits have to flee, including the 'Spirit of Infirmity' which holds so many people in captivity, today. This powerful praise and worship to God drives out Satan and allows us to be able to interface with God in a very intimate way. And the unsaved, cannot help but be touched by such power and intimacy, as they observe God pouring out His mercy and grace upon His people. Because although their hearts have not yet recognised Jesus Christ, as their Saviour, they are still made in God's image and cannot help but recognise the powerful Presence of God, as He extends love to His people in this beautiful and intimate way.

This wonderful connection established between ourselves and God, our Father, through praise and worship, is shown again and again in the Bible. King David was a man after God's own heart, as is confirmed in: (1 Samuel 13:14) when Samuel was speaking to King Saul and said: "But now thy kingdom shall not continue: the Lord hath sought him, a man after his own heart, and the Lord hath commanded him to be captain over his people, because thou hast not kept that which the Lord commanded thee" Beloved, David loved God and His commandments with all of His heart and loved to Praise God with singing, dancing, and with instruments. David was "a man after God's own heart" in that he was truly thankful. He is credited with writing over 50 Psalms and said in one of them, "I wash my hands in innocence, and go about your altar, O LORD, proclaiming aloud your praise and telling of all your wonderful deeds" (Psalm 26:6–7). David's life was marked by seasons of great peace and prosperity, as well as times of fear and despair. But through all the seasons in his life, he never forgot to thank the Lord for everything that he had through praise. This was truly one of David's finest characteristics; because He knew the power of praise and worship and in one Psalm, He expresses this beautifully by saying: "Enter His gates with thanksgiving, and His courts with praise! Give thanks to Him; bless His name!" (Psalm 100:4, ESV). As followers of Jesus Christ beloved, we must follow David's example by offering praise through thanksgiving to God, as this will bring joy and breakthrough into our lives.

The simple truth is, that there is power in our acknowledgement that God is worthy, above all else. His Spirit urges us onward, to press in close to Him. It truly doesn't matter how musical or not so musical we feel like we are, and it really doesn't matter if we like upbeat praise, more reflective worship songs, or traditional hymns. It doesn't matter if we're alone, with a few, or indeed are in a large group. To be honest, it doesn't even matter whether we "feel" like engaging in praise and worship or not. What matters is this – that our hearts are lifted up to Him in thankfulness; so that we can commune with our Creator and King.

**So, Let Us Examine How Praise and Worship Helps in Our Relationship with God, our Father:**

1. Praise gets our focus off ourselves and back onto God. Beloved, in our often "selfie" focused world, we need this constant reminder, that life is not all about us. We may know this truth deep within our spirits (our hearts),

as Christians; but our soul realm (our minds and emotions) often think differently a lot of the time. Let's face it, we are all prone to selfishness. But God desires our eyes to be firmly fixed upon Him, because He knows this is where our true hope can be found. He is worthy of our praise, beloved, no matter what we face from day to day. God's Word says: "Praise Him for His mighty deeds; praise Him according to his excellent greatness!" (Psalm 150:2); "And my tongue shall speak of your righteousness and of your praise all day long." (Psalm 35:28).

2. Praise brings us to a place of humility. Beloved, through praising God we remember our dependency upon Him, as we acknowledge our need for Him. And as we praise Him, as our Creator and King, we then admit and recognize that we're not in control, but He is; and that He is above all. His Word says: "Let us come into his presence with thanksgiving; let us make a joyful noise to Him with songs of praise! For the Lord is a great God, and a great King above all gods." (Psalm.95:2-3), "I will give you thanks in the great congregation: I will praise you among much people." (Psalm 35:18)

3. Praise makes the enemy flee. Beloved, praise to God truly pushes back the darkness that surrounds us and blocks the attacks of Satan and even blocks every lie spoken against us. Believe me, evil has "to vacate the premises" if we're praising our God; because 'God inhabits the praises of His people' as is written in (Psalm 22:3). In

fact, in the story of Jehoshaphat, we see God miraculously defeated the enemy, because of the people's obedience to praise Him in (2 Chronicles 20:22): "As they began to sing and praise, the Lord set ambushes against the men of Ammon and Moab and Mount Seir, who were invading Judah, and they were defeated."

4. Praise leaves no room for complaining and negativity. Sometimes even within our prayers, we can tend to complain about our problems. God knows our hearts. And He cares about all that concerns us. But through praise, we're focused on Him, no longer allowing too much attention to be centred upon our own struggles. And then we are reminded of what He has already done in our lives. We are also reminded that He knows what concerns us and is fully capable of taking care of any and all problems that burden us. (Psalm 103:2-4) says: "Bless the Lord, O my soul, and forget not all His benefits, who forgives all your iniquity, who heals all your diseases, who redeems your life from the pit, who crowns you with steadfast love and mercy."

5. Praise makes room for God's blessings over our lives. Beloved, God, our Father; will not withhold His goodness from us, and praise does open up a wonderful doorway of blessing in the Spirit Realm; as we come into the Presence of our King. (Ephesians 1:3) confirms this by saying: "Blessed be the God and Father of our Lord Jesus Christ, who has blessed us with all spiritual blessings in heavenly places in Christ:"

6. Praise invites His presence. God draws near to us when we praise Him and we remember what His Precious Son, Jesus Christ did for us on the cross by His sacrifice, which was written about by His disciple Peter in (1 Peter 2:9): "But you are a chosen generation, a royal priesthood, an holy nation, a peculiar people; that you should show forth the praises of Him who has called you out of darkness into His marvellous light."

7. Our spirits are refreshed and renewed in His Presence. Beloved, when we praise God we are strengthened by His peace and refuelled by His wonderful anointing of grace and joy, as is shown in these wonderful Bible verses. And "In His presence, there is fullness of joy." (Psalm 16:11): "Because your love is better than life, my lips will glorify you. I will praise you as long as I live, and in your Name, I will lift up my hands." (Psalm 63:3-4)

8. It releases God's Holy Power so that miracles happen. Beloved, people's lives are affected and changed, and hearts are transformed through praise and worship; and God causes a great shaking to happen amongst His people. This is shown clearly in (Acts 16:25-26) where it says: "As Paul and Silas sat in prison, shackled, and chained, they kept right on praising God. And God sent an earthquake that shook the cells and broke the chains. The jailer and all his family came to know Christ that very night. "

Beloved, this book is about becoming" Fighting Fit for the Latter Days," and engaging in praise and worship, each and every day, is a good way to ensure that your hearts stay humble and that you are intimately connected with God, the Father, as you navigate through life,. In this modern day world of technology, there is no room for excuses like "you cannot praise the Lord, because you don't play an instrument or you cannot sing," for there are any number of wonderful praise and worship songs, that can be accessed via the internet, through just one touch of your finger. Beloved, take this necessary step, and get connected with the Lord of Lords and the King of Kings, through praise and worship and spending intimate time with the Lord, and your life will be changed forever, Amen!

# Chapter 19

# The Marvelous Benefit of Staying Active

As a person prone to sitting behind a computer, because of my love of writing, I am aware of the sedentary position this places me in. And I know also, that because of the unlikelihood of me engaging in much daily activity, whilst I am writing, that I must ensure I endeavour to be as active as I can, to ensure my health does not suffer. Beloved, God's Word says in (1 Corinthians 9:26-27): "Do you not know that in a race all the runners run; but only one receives the prize? So, run that you may obtain it. Every athlete exercises self-control in all things. They do it to receive a perishable wreath, but we an imperishable. So, I do not run aimlessly; I do not box as one beating the air. But I discipline my body and keep it under control, lest after preaching to others I myself should be disqualified." Beloved, God wants us to safeguard our bodies through discipline, and if we are not staying active and ensuring we are getting enough exercise though the week; then we are in effect, as the scripture says: either "running aimlessly," or indeed "boxing in the air."

Beloved, there are severe risks to a sedentary lifestyle and with this being the case; we should do everything possible to remain active. First, you, may be wondering what we are referring to when we mention a 'sedentary lifestyle.' Well, a sedentary lifestyle is defined as a type of lifestyle where an individual does not receive regular amounts of physical activity. And in the secular world, this is where physical inactivity is considered 'the failure to meet the recommendations of the Center for Disease Control (CDC),' stating: "that an individual should participate in a minimum of 150 minutes of moderate exercise, or 75 minutes of a more vigorous regimen daily."

Most health professionals are also in agreement that walking 10,000 steps a day (approximately 5 miles) is the ideal goal to set for improving health and reducing the health risks caused by inactivity; although frankly, even half way towards that goal could make a huge difference in someone's life. In fact, according to the World Health Organization (WHO), 60 to 85% of the population worldwide do not engage in enough activity; which makes physical inactivity; the fourth leading risk factor for premature death globally.

The good news is, that this doesn't have to be your fate. And although, the general workplace trend is headed towards a more sedentary setting, as machines continue to replace jobs; which require more activity, you don't have to submit to that. In fact, the easiest way to increase activity levels may be achieved in or around the workplace, a place in which the average individual spends up to eight or more hours sitting per day.

This may be possible, by simply trying to find different ways to travel to work for a start; and then by doing a few exercises either early in the morning or at night, which can significantly reduce the effects caused by inactivity. And beloved, within two weeks; people generally become used to this increase in exercise, and this soon becomes a part of their daily routine. You just have to give increased activity a chance and it can make all the difference.

Beloved, because we are in the latter days, God requires us to be in tip top shape; so that we do not open doors for sickness or other demonic attacks. In the bible, there was much need for the people of God to remain physically fit; because of the readiness required to fight battles and hunt for food. And the shepherds walked the fields endlessly, as they drove the sheep and defended them against lions, and other wild animals.

The escalating rate of obesity in the U.S. is just one example of how Satan can use the combination of the sin of gluttony and a sedentary lifestyle to shorten the lives of God's people. (Philippians 3:19) talks about the devastating effects of food greed or gluttony; and says this: "Their end is destruction, their god is their belly, and they glory in their shame, with minds set on earthly things."

But there is a much larger, more encompassing issue at hand of which obesity is just one symptom. This issue in fact, beloved, is a growing occurrence of disease and addiction in men and women, as the demonic spirits enter in and attach themselves to our bodies and souls due to our lack of discipline and wilful disobedience. The effects of this terrible stronghold is devastating, as people succumb to the temptation of food, drugs, or alcohol, again and again.

Beloved, if you find you have gone down this route, there is hope in God, if you repent of your sinful behaviour patterns, and you work towards building up your discipline. This increase of discipline can be achieved as you strengthen yourself in God's Word and communicate with God, the

Father, who loves you so dearly, For only then, can these Spirits be cast out and the door to the Spirit of Gluttony be firmly closed forever.

As a minister, I have counselled many people with these types of issues through the years, and it has always been imperative that we looked at all of the connected and contributing factors, which resulted in the gluttonous, sedentary lifestyle, they found themselves in; for some of these behaviour patterns and strongholds went back to their early childhood years.

One such case, I remember quite clearly, was when a woman came to my church office, many years ago and said to me: "I think I have a spirit of fat and tired, and I can't go on unless something is done about it" The woman only came occasionally to church; but I could see from the desperate look upon her face, that she needed my help very badly. After a series of weekly counselling sessions, I determined she had grown up with a very critical mother and then ended up with a very critical husband. The woman was terribly obese and hardly stepped out of her home most days; except when she had to, and food was her comfort day and night.

This poor woman was suffering; but I knew she could not be free of her addiction to food, unless her self-esteem improved, and she was able to get her eyes fixed upon God and His great love for her. And so I started talking to her not about her problems; but rather about how she was made in God's image and that He loved her so much, that He had sent His Son to die on the cross for her, so that she could have eternal life and live victoriously every single day. I also started talking to her about letting the joy of the Lord be her strength, not food. And I began encouraging her to pray more and to read the word, and to listen to worship music; and gradually, ever so gradually, I could see the woman's wonderful transformation happen, right before my eyes.

You see beloved, people just need to know that they are loved and treasured by God; and that if they have Him to lean upon, when things are hard...then obesity and addictions became a thing of the past. The truth is, once they come to the realisation that they don't need food or alcohol, or whatever the addiction might be, because they have something a million times better in God, the entire identity of that person changes as they become sons and daughters of the Living God.. Beloved, in reference to that dear lady, it wasn't long, only a few short months later, when she started losing weight and engaging in exercise. And by the end of the year, that same woman was a happy, vibrant woman and was an active member of our church, Hallelujah!

# Chapter 20

## How God Restores Us Through Time

Beloved, I once heard a type of popular Christian counselling method described as "quick and fun;" and I nearly cried as this description was spoken about so haphazardly, over an Internet Podcast that could potentially reach millions of people around the world. I have experienced a fair amount of pain in my own life, and have helped countless others through Christian counselling, and beloved, I just don't believe that deep rooted pain developed over years of a person's life can be dealt with so quickly and so easily.

Now, I am not saying that the power of God can't intervene instantly in our circumstances, for He is great and mighty, and fully able to do so. But years of experience have taught me that we, as human beings; are complex creations of the Almighty God, and in order to understand and walk freely in His grace, from the things or people that have hurt or hindered us so desperately, we need time to reflect upon our circumstances, and time to repent of our sins and to forgive others. We also need time to put into action solutions given to us by the Holy Spirit, and Spirit filled men and women of God; whose chief goal is to humbly submit to their purpose and calling in God; as they wield considerable influence in our lives.

Beloved, as I have said countless times in this book, "we are made in God's image" and because of this wonderful fact, we tend to use our reasoning to help ourselves to understand why something has happened to us; and what we can do to protect or free ourselves from our troubles. God understands this need, and advocates that this thought process is acceptable to Him and confirms this in His Word, which says in Isaiah 1:18: "Come now, let us reason together," says the LORD: "though your sins are like scarlet, they shall be as white as snow; though they are red like crimson, like wool." God, the Father wants us to understand why we need to repent, and how such repentance and forgiveness can lead to complete healing and restoration.

God has great regard for time and as mentioned before in Chapter one, He most certainly has allotted seasons for all things. This is particularly important to keep in mind, in regards to miracles and healing; for although miracles are brought about in a spontaneous manner by the Holy Spirit, and are usually brought about for the purpose of providing a great witness of God's power and compassion to the unsaved. Healings in regard to physical ailments or disease or mental torment can be far more complex; and may involve any number of combinations of sin conditions and demonic clusterings of oppression and is, without a doubt; brought about by an open door caused by wilful disobedience of God's laws.

And with this being the case, many Christians walk in so much condemnation, that they can't seem to muster enough faith to receive God's compassion or healing power, or equally Christians (either consciously or subconsciously), seek to deflect attention from their own sin conditions, and they often judge and condemn their fellow Christians, so that they too, have such low self-esteem, that they can't receive God's healing power either. But God's word says "there is no condemnation through Christ Jesus" in (Romans 8:1). Praise God!

Beloved, if we need healing, then our tender and loving Father, God; does not only want us to receive it; but He wants us to learn from the experience; so that we never have to "walk through that valley" again. And if we are open, He will indeed teach us, how to walk in perfect peace, as we take authority over this demonic attack which has taken over our lives. (Mark 13:34) says: "For the Son of Man is as a man taking a far journey, who left his house, and gave authority to his servants, and to every man his work, and commanded the porter to watch." He gave AUTHORITY to his servants and to every man his work. Authority means the right to command obedience, the right to enforce obedience, and the right to act officially. Christ has authority over sickness and the devil. He has the right to command the sickness to leave and the devil has to obey. He has the right to enforce obedience, and He has the right to act in the official capacity, as the Son of God.

The centurion came to Jesus, and said, "My servant is sick at home and I want you to heal him." And Jesus said, "I will go." The centurion said, "Jesus, you don't need to go and heal him, I am not worthy that you should enter under my roof but speak the Word and my servant will be healed." He said, "I am a man of authority. The ones over me tell me what to do and I must obey. I have authority over a hundred men. I will tell them to do this or do that and they do what I command them to do." And he said, "Now Christ, you have authority. You don't need to come to my home, all you have to do is say the Word and that sickness will have to leave because you have authority over it." And Jesus marvelled and said, "I have not found such great faith, not in all Israel." (Paraphrased from Luke 7:3-9).

The thing that brought healing to that centurion's servant was his faith in the authority that there was in the Name of Jesus over that sickness. And today, if you have faith in the authority of the Name of Jesus over sickness, you will most assuredly be healed; but give the Lord time to do a great work in you at the same time. The very moment that you appropriate that faith you will be healed; but the physical manifestation may linger until your faith is strengthened or indeed the other areas of your life are dealt with, and repentance or indeed forgiveness happens. So, you may well ask, how do I remain in perfect peace until the manifestation comes?

The Word of God says, "Perfect Love casts out fear," in (1 John 4:18). Now, I understand (because I have been there), and I know, how physical symptoms or indeed worries can cause you to doubt that God can and will heal you. But truly believing and understanding God's perfect love for you is the key, and this will carry you to such a wonderful place of peace and faith, that in time you will be able to embrace the marvellous truth "that nothing is impossible with God," as is stated in (Matthew 19:26).

The Apostle Paul talks about God's great love for us, in (Ephesians 3:16-21), and says: "I pray that from His glorious, unlimited resources He will empower you with inner strength through His Spirit. Then Christ will make His home in your hearts as you trust in Him. Your roots will grow down into God's love and keep you strong. And may you have the power to understand, as all God's people should, how wide, how long, how high, and how deep His love is. May you experience the love of Christ, though it is too great to understand fully. Then you will be made complete with all the fullness of life and power that comes from God." Amen.

Now Jesus gave His disciples the same authority over sickness and demonic oppression that He walked in, and in (Luke 9:1), it says, "He called His twelve disciples together, and gave them power and authority over all devils, and to cure diseases." Jesus said they were to preach the kingdom of God and to heal the sick. And in (Matthew 10:8), it says: Jesus told His disciples, "Heal the sick, cleanse the lepers, raise the dead, cast out devils: freely ye have received, freely give." Yet, some people say we shouldn't preach on healing at all. But beloved, Jesus preached and practiced healing. The disciples preached and practiced healing. And the Word of God speaks often about the wonderful healings and miracles that took place in the Name of Jesus. So we must embrace the fact, that Jesus not only gave His disciples the power and authority to heal the sick and set the captives free; but He gave them a mandate to go about "spreading the gospel unto all the earth," as is spoken about in (Mark 16:15): which they fulfilled by the teaching of the gospel and the establishment of the New Testament churches.

And during this time, they were teaching the new converts of the New Testament churches to understand about repentance of their sins and forgiveness. But they were also teaching about how healing comes about and how they could stay free from sickness and oppression in their everyday lives. So, as well as prayers of healing, these blessed people of the New Testament Churches were gaining priceless understanding and wisdom to help them in their journey as children of the Living God.

(Ephesians 1:18) speaks about this beautifully and says: "I pray that the eyes of your heart may be enlightened in order that you may know the hope to which He has called you, the riches of His glorious inheritance." Beloved, let your eyes of understanding be opened to truth, as you believe God for your healing in the Precious Name of Jesus, Amen.

# Chapter 21

## The Importance of Balanced Relationships

Beloved, often as a Christian you will find, that as a child of God you are in total contrast to the ways of the world; and the ungodly people that live within it. And as a result, you may find that it is very challenging to have balanced relationships in your workplace or indeed in other environments, you may take part in. I, myself, have in times past, fallen into the trap of setting my expectations too high; and hence, I have expected people to act in a certain way, (according to God's principles); and have been terribly disappointed, when they have not met my expectations. Beloved, it is ridiculous to expect people who are unsaved to act according to God's principles. It is equally unrealistic for us to have any expectations at all beloved, in regard to the saved or unsaved people of this world. For we are not God, and frankly; we do not have the right to judge others. God's Word confirms this, in (Matthew 7:1-5), which says: 1 "Do not judge, or you too will be judged. For in the same way you judge others, you will be judged, and with the measure you use, it will be measured to you." Why do you look at the speck of sawdust in your brother's eye and pay no attention to the plank in your own eye?" "How can you say to your brother, 'Let me take the speck out of your eye,' when all the time there is a plank in your own eye?" "You hypocrite, first take the plank out of your own eye, and then you will see clearly to remove the speck from your brother's eye." Beloved, these sound like harsh words; but Jesus wanted to ensure we knew this is absolutely not the way to live our lives victoriously, or to bring the lost into the Kingdom of God.

In fact, beloved, the religious spirit that many Christians harbour in their hearts, is a demonic spirit that attacks many men and women of God and attaches itself to their minds and emotions. This occurs, because a door swings wide open, due to people participating in the sins of self-righteousness pride, and fear of anything or anyone different to themselves. This is a toxic sin condition, that can place a choke hold upon a church and will stunt its' growth and spiritual freedom, like very few other tactics of the enemy can. God' word says in (2 Corinthians 3:17): "Now the Lord is the Spirit, and where the Spirit of the Lord is, there is freedom." And anything that stops the freedom of the Holy Spirit or indeed the love and acceptance of one person for another, is most certainly not of God. Now Beloved, God does not advocate that we accept the sin; but we can accept the person who is carrying the sin and walk in love towards them without judging them. This is depicted in the bible when Jesus after having rid Mary Magdalene of seven demons, received her as one of His most faithful followers during His years of ministry upon the earth.

Beloved, we most redesign the way we look at things, and not trust what the world says about people, we have relationships with. It is very important instead, that we look at people through the eyes of Jesus, showing love and compassion towards others. This is true of all relationships, whether they are family, church, or relationships in the outside world. For if

God loves us unconditionally, and we are made in His image, then we must follow the example of our Father in Heaven.

Yet, there is a condition that God talks about in His Word, where we are advised not to be, "unequally yoked," with unbelievers. (2 Corinthians 6:14), says: "Do not be unequally yoked together with unbelievers. For what do righteousness and wickedness have in common? Or what fellowship can light have with darkness?" So, you may ask, what does being unequally yoked mean, and how does that affect our relationships with others? Well beloved, the definition of a "yoke" is 'a joining of two individuals together or a binding agreement.' And so, to be joined in this manner would have to denote that these two individuals would be going in the same direction and have the same goals.

There are many types of yokes or commitments we have in life; such as: marriage, the rearing of our children, friendships or business relationships. And God knew the danger of darkness that could be introduced when mixing the righteous with the unrighteous, for temptation and sin can enter our lives so quietly, with our senses so dulled, that we can no longer recognise what is sin and what is not sin. And when we step outside God's clearly defined boundaries, disappointment and grief are sure to be brought to the forefront in these relationships, when God is no longer at the centre of our lives.

In fact, in the past few decades of my own ministry, I have witnessed one of Satan's most effective plans in wiping out young believers; and that has been through the "Unequal Yoking," of these young believers to unbelievers, who are actively participating in sin. Sadly, I have seen many bright and enthusiastic Christians, who have become caught up in this subtle snare, and have, for all intents and purposes, ruined their whole life and testimony for God, as their loyalties have become divided between their commitment to God and their ungodly spouses.

Beloved, I am not saying that these ungodly spouses cannot be prayed into the Kingdom of God; but this must be their choice and their heart decision; and oftentimes, it is difficult for them, as they see the frailties and inevitable shortcomings of their Christian spouses, which makes it hard for them to see the benefits of such a commitment.

So, let us examine, how we as Christians can be unequally yoked according to the Word of God:

- The Social Yoke is the unequal yoke with unconverted companions. The Word says: "Know ye not that the friendship of the world is enmity with God? Whosoever, therefore, will be a friend of the world is the enemy of God" (James 4:4). "If any man love the world, the love of the Father is not in him" (1 John 2:15).

- The Matrimonial Yoke, or the "Unequal Yoke," in marriage. "Neither shalt thou make marriages with them; thy daughter thou shalt not give unto his son, nor his daughter shalt thou take unto thy son. For they will turn away thy son from following me, that they may serve other gods: so, will the anger of the LORD be kindled against you, and destroy thee suddenly" (Deuteronomy 7:3-4). To the saints of the present age the Word is equally explicit, "Be ye not unequally yoked together with unbelievers" (2 Corinthians 6:14); and "Married…only in the Lord" (1 Corinthians 7:39).

- The Commercial Yoke, or the "Unequal Yoke," in business. "Thou shalt not plough with an ox and an [donkey] together" (Deuteronomy 22:10). We are also told in the bible that "Whatsoever ye do, in word or deed, do all in the name of the Lord Jesus" (Colossians 3:17); and "Whatsoever ye do, do all to the glory of God" (1 Corinthians 10:31).
- The Religious Yoke, or the 'Unequal Yoke," in the worship and service of God. The wheat and tares, or the children of God and the children of the devil, will both grow together in the field (and the field is the world) until the end (see Matt 13:24-30, 38, 39); but they are not to be yoked together in the church, or associated in the worship and service of God. We read of the early church that "all that believed were together," and "of the rest durst no man join himself to them" (Acts 2:44; 5:13).

Beloved, we must guard our hearts (spirits) from ungodly ties that can rain destruction upon us in countless ways. There is a humanistic mindset that promotes the idea of total acceptance of others and their practices, no matter how evil those practices might be. And this "Live and let live" attitude has led to the ushering in of flagrantly, sinful laws in modern day countries around the world; which are an abomination to God. These laws support gay rights and abortion, and many other sinful agendas, and have taken over all forms of literature, television, art, the internet, and fashion industries; altering mindsets so dramatically, that this evil is accepted as normal. And when God's laws are raised up as the real truth, they are cast down and called antiquated and not in touch with the modern-day world.

So, what does this have to do with having a balanced relationship, well everything. For although you can accept and love someone, you must not accept the sin "as part of the package." And until they have a true commitment to God, you must stay disciplined and not walk with them on the road of sin and death. (Proverbs 13:20), says: "Walk with the wise and become wise, for a companion of fools suffers harm."

Beloved, if you already have loved ones within your family, that are not committed to God." Then there is hope for you, because you do have the legal right to pray for them to be blessed and to be saved and brought into the Kingdom of God, for God's word promises this in: (Acts 16:31), which says, And they replied, "Believe in the Lord Jesus, and you will be saved, you and your household."

Most assuredly, we have a compassionate and loving God, but He cannot abide or accept sin, for His Precious Son, Jesus Christ, made the supreme sacrifice and died brutally to take the sins of the world (our sins), there with Him, which has given us victory over every sickness, sorrow, and sin. And the way beloved, to have a fulfilled and victorious life, ensuring balanced relationships, is to accept what He has done for us; and to walk with humility and love towards others. Then, as we obey God's laws, and aspire to live a holy and righteous life, we will have spiritual eyes to see and understand God's love and plan for our lives, remaining wise and vigilant in everything we do, as Peter advises in 1 Peter 5:8 "Be sober, be vigilant; because your adversary the devil walks about like a roaring lion, seeking whom he may devour." Amen.

# Chapter 22

## The Power of Praying with God's Word

Beloved, remember that God's Word is the 'Sword of the Spirit;' and if we are going to get results with our prayers, then we must read God's Word and use it as a powerful resource. (Hebrews 4:12), says: "For the Word of God is quick, and powerful, and sharper than any two-edged sword, piercing even to the dividing asunder of soul and spirit, and of the joints and marrow, and is a discerner of the thoughts and intents of the heart." What this scripture means beloved, is that you can put God's Word to work, and that it has the power to divide the spirit realm from the soul realm; and so any demonic spirit that seeks to influence our minds or emotions or indeed our mental health, just doesn't stand a chance, Hallelujah!

Jesus was passionate about the Word of God; and he certainly used it when He prayed. You see, He knew the Power of the Word of God in intercession. This was, without a doubt, put to the test when He was tempted by the devil in the wilderness. And to get the victory over the devil; He simply quoted the Word of God; and because of the Mighty Power of this action, the devil was soundly defeated and had to flee.

During His time in the wilderness, Jesus showed us, through His own example, how speaking the Word of God can bring exciting breakthroughs for us, as we implement it into our prayer life, during the most difficult times of spiritual attack.

Praying this way, powerfully fights against any battles we may have in this life. In fact, by using the spiritual weapon of God's Word, we remind Satan and his minions, of the authority we walk in, as adopted sons and daughters of the Most High God. This authority in the supernatural realm is so powerful, beloved; that it actually pulls down demonic strongholds (2 Corinthians 10:3-5). In fact, the action of using God's Word in prayer, stalwartly negates any agreement we previously have had with darkness; (whether consciously or unconsciously); and aligns us fully with God, and His divine plan for our lives. And furthermore, praying and using God's Word brings freedom, discernment, and protection. in all aspects of our lives.

Beloved, as a minister I have been attacked from time to time by the Spirit of Poverty. And whilst, I was pastoring my second church, I was living in a mobile home, which we had placed on the church property for I and my family's use. But the problem was, there was no septic tank; which meant our toilet within the mobile home, was of no use to us, whatsoever. This also meant every time we needed to use the toilet, we had to go across to the church. Now beloved, I can remember many long, cold walks in the winter time; which was an especially onerous task, because my daughter, who was only five years old at the time, needed at least one to two nightly trips across to the church, rain or shine.

And so, as we faced this dilemma, I started petitioning God in prayer using His Word. To petition means 'to request something which is desired, in a respectful and humble way, to a superior or to one, who is in authority.' And a petition is most effective when we use the Lord's Word to make our requests.

Beloved, the scripture I set before God, my Father, day and night was: "The lions may grow weak and hungry but those who seek the Lord lack no good thing. (Psalm 34:10 NIV). Now, this may seem like a simple scripture; but beloved, it was powerful, because only three weeks later, a man I didn't know, but who said he knew me, and had attended a few prophetic meetings at our church, knocked on my door and said he felt led of the Lord to give me money. He then proceeded to hand over to me a large, brown paper bag, absolutely filled up to the brim with cash money.

I protested and told him, "I couldn't possibly take such a large amount of money from him." But he took off his hat and placed it on his heart and replied, "Please Mam, the Lord has been waking me up every night, and telling me to give this here money, that my mother left me when she died, to you; and I would really like to get some sleep tonight." Apparently, the Lord had been waking him up every single night for three weeks and had been telling him to give the inheritance money to that little blonde pastor on the hill! Hallelujah! Now beloved, I had also been using this scripture to ask God to help me; so I could buy a plane ticket too, so I could go and make a gospel record; as He had opened a wonderful door and a Nashville record producer had offered me a record deal a few months earlier. And miraculously, the amount the man gave me was the exact amount I needed, to dig a septic tank for our mobile home; and to pay my expenses for that trip. Praise God! Now that is the provision of God and I believe was entirely granted; because of my prayer and petitioning with God's Word. Now beloved, that does not make God, some sort of Santa Claus, ready to grant our every request, if we are good.

But He will meet you in your hour of need and bring forth His provision, in alignment with His Word. Hallelujah!

You see beloved, there is no great mystery to intercession; because really it is profoundly simple. You just tell God how much you love Him as you come into His Presence, and humbly present your need or request to Him in the 'Courts of Heaven,' and quote what God says in His Word; and as long as it is aligned with His purposes for Your life, and you are clean before Him, in reference to sin conditions or generational curses; then there will be no legal reason for God to withhold blessings and you will get powerful results. Because God loves it, when we agree with Him through His Word. And those of us who read His Word faithfully, know how the Holy Spirit speaks to us through it. And as we pray it back to Him; with the Holy Spirit leading us, then only good things can come our way, as a result. This is confirmed in Isaiah 30:18 which says: "Yet the Lord longs to be gracious to you; therefore, He will rise up to show you compassion. For the Lord is a God of justice. Blessed are all who wait for Him." When we pray God's Word, beloved, it transforms us on the inside; and believe me, it truly changes us for the better and builds us up immensely. This simple act causes us to unite with God's heart in the most amazing and reassuring way.

And to make matters even better, praying God's Word gives us the strength to stand, until we get our breakthrough. Also, the wonderful revelation we get from Him, through His Word strengthens us, in the soul realm, as our mind and emotions are moved by His life-giving promises. Beloved, we can even change whole cities when we agree with God's heart in prayer. For as we pray, the power and anointing of the Holy Spirit is released and revival is established in that city, in a very real and lifechanging way. So, if you are discouraged, you will feel markedly different after God speaks to your heart through His Word? It's as if a light suddenly goes on that dispels all the darkness. This is because God upholds all things by the Word of His Power, which is spoken about in (Hebrew 1:3). "The Son is the radiance of God's glory and the exact representation of His being, sustaining all things by His Powerful Word. After He had provided purification for sins, He sat down at the right hand of the Majesty of God in heaven."

Prayers in the Bible are easy to find. There are many types; for example, there are the Psalms, the Prayers of Wisdom in the book of Proverbs, the Song of Songs, the Prayers of the Prophets, the Prayers of Jesus, the Apostolic Prayers, and the Hymns of Revelations. But I would encourage you to find a bible verse that fits your prayer need, beloved; and to just stand upon it and bring it up to God (as you pray), raising up a petition respectfully, and saying to the Lord... that the answering of your prayer need lines up with His Word. This then, makes it an open dialogue beloved, between you and Him, and He will answer through actions or through His still, small voice, believe me.

I would also urge you to put that scripture, you are standing upon, on every mirror in your house and even on your refrigerator, as you submit your prayer need to God, so that every time you see that scripture, you are lifting your need up to Him as a petition. Praying by using the Word of God, will have a dramatic effect upon your prayer life and in prayer meetings. And it is definitely a key to the success of your prayers, as you get true breakthrough for your life, as well.

This type of prayer life will take you to such a higher level in your relationship with God, the Father, that your faith will increase and rise up to a new place in authoritative strength, as you pray the will of God and see answers to your prayers again and again. This is confirmed in (1 John 5:14-15), which says: "This is the confidence we have in approaching God: that if we ask anything according to His will, He hears us. And if we know that He hears us—whatever we ask—we know that we have what we asked of Him." Amen.

# Chapter 23

## The Power of the Prophetic Word

Everyone's life can be fast forwarded by the prophetic word. In fact, with a prophetic word, God can give you a momentum for the future like you never had before. You see beloved, in the realm of the Spirit there are things that belong to you; and by the power and influence of a prophetic word; you can take possession, of what belongs to you; because God has ordained it to be yours, as His child. Remember, that Saul was just an ordinary peasant herding donkeys, when he came into contact with the prophet Samuel. But when the prophet revealed to him the mind of God concerning his life, everything changed for that simple peasant, 365 degrees. You see prophetic words can convey the 'Mind of God' in an instant. And in Saul's case, the peasant was transformed from a common man into a king of Israel, after the word was spoken over his life.

Beloved, many people are walking through life without knowing the true purpose of God or destiny that He has for their lives. They are in fact, just experiencing life as it happens, rather than grabbing hold of their God-given destiny and truly living out a purposeful existence. And sadly, some may never discover the purpose of God concerning their lives until a prophet comes along. The Word of God talks about us, as Christians; being anointed for a purpose in (2 Corinthians 1: 21-22), which says: "Now it is God who makes both us and you stand firm in Christ.

He anointed us, set his seal of ownership on us, and put his Spirit in our hearts, as a deposit, guaranteeing what is to come." These two scripture verses are quite significant, as they speak about the power we have to not only "stand firm in Christ," but that God has "anointed and sealed us as His," so that we have His protection, as we walk under the anointing of the Spirit of God.

The anointing is the 'Presence of God' which lifts a person from the realm of the ordinary into the realm of the extraordinary. It is about divinity having a spiritual interaction with humanity, in order to introduce the principles and the power of God, that makes a man or woman walk and talk like God; and we must understand beloved, that when a man or woman is anointed; that they actually carry the very characteristics and nature of God, as they flow under His Spirit, and this is how you will know that they are true sons and daughters of the Living God. For His love, grace, and compassion, will take the predominant place in their hearts always, despite the fact, that they are human beings that deal with their own foibles and struggles themselves from day to day. Beloved, when Elisha was walking with Elijah, he saw the grace upon Elijah and he desired a double portion of that grace, even though Elijah had his human side too. And because of Elisha's heartfelt desire he received the double anointing upon his life; and fantastically, he began doing humanly impossible things, far surpassing anything that Elijah did.

The prophetic word is a divinely inspired Word of God, anointed and charged by the Holy Spirit; which carries the Power of God that can transform lives and entire situations. Every genuine prophetic word has its' very foundations rooted in God. In (Genesis 1:1), it says, God spoke the word "and God said." This means beloved, that God spoke 'His Word' into existence.

Which means, that anytime a prophetic word comes into your life, that you must realise that it is the divinely inspired word of God, which has the power to move you into the future and indeed change your present. The prophetic word is all about hearing the voice of the Holy Spirit, and then, speaking it into existence; as you impact nations, communities, and whole groups of people, as formerly, hopeless situations are then aligned gloriously with God's purposes. A prophetic word is the declaration of the voice of the Holy Spirit that reveals the mind, heart, and the purpose of God concerning you.

Now beloved, this may mean the prophetic word may come about in several forms which may include correction, instruction, encouragement and even reproof to the body of Christ. Joseph was a great example of this when he spoke a prophetic word into the life of King Pharaoh, and because of his disobedience, great destruction came upon Egypt. The prophetic word is also the word that is established by God as a channel of blessings, and can be a glorious voice of revelation which declares the mind of Christ concerning His body(church); or for that matter; any agenda upon the face of the earth. When God communicates His purposes through His prophetic ministers, then He will indeed execute His plan.

Prophetic ministers will most definitely have direction and instructions for others as God ordains. And such instructions can birth signs, wonders, and miracles. A 'God example' is when Jesus met a man who was born blind and He gave him a direction and an instruction which brought about his healing. (John 9;1-8). Elisha also gave a prophetic direction and instruction to Naaman the Syrian to go and wash in the river Jordan and he received his healing (2 Kings5;1-7). Praise God!

# Chapter 24

## When Life Isn't Fair!

Beloved, I was born and raised in America, and I can attest to the fact, that both men and women in that great country are raised to be strong and very vocal about most things. And to be honest, standing up for your rights is considered, a very admirable thing to do there. And certainly, if you are a parent of children old enough to speak, (no matter what country, you happen to live in), you would have heard them complain and say, "But that isn't fair!" And you then would have responded, "Life isn't fair!" Beloved, most of us are born with a strong innate sense of justice and have an intense desire to fight for our rights, when we have been treated unfairly. Which seems a contradiction in terms, for if we know that life isn't fair, then why do we fight back when we're the victims of unfair treatment?

So, let's assume beloved, that you are a conscientious worker on your job. You get to work early, you're careful not to extend your lunch breaks, and sometimes you stay late on your own time to finish a job. You're also very careful not to waste company time with excessive talking to your co-workers. You, in addition, work very hard for the company; but because you're a Christian, you don't go out drinking after hours with the boss and you certainly don't swap the latest dirty jokes with him. However, another worker is, in your opinion, "a total waste of space." He often comes in late; he spends a lot of time chatting with the secretaries, he takes long lunches, and he does makes loads of errors in his work, which you often have to correct. But he also goes out drinking with the boss and he always has a new dirty joke that causes the boss to have a good laugh. This causes you to feel that the boss favours your co-worker over you. And in time, you are proven right, when a promotion opens up, and he gets the better job and you are overlooked.

Life isn't fair! The important question is, "How do you respond when you're treated unfairly?" "How should you respond?" "Is it wrong to defend yourself or to stand up for your rights?" "And how exactly should a Christian respond when treated unfairly, especially on the job?" Beloved, this is the question Peter addresses in (1 Peter 2:18-23).

And the truth is, you won't like his answer. (I can guess that; because I don't like his answer much either!) But regardless, his answer is: "When treated unfairly by a superior, we should submissively endure by entrusting ourselves to God, the Righteous Judge."

Beloved, that statement is more easily said, then it is to carry out. So, how exactly can we carry out a modern-day re-enactment of Peter's words; when they were actually meant for slaves? Do these things apply beyond the realm of employment and onto any situation? And is it always wrong to defend ourselves or to speak out when we are treated unfairly? Also, are Christians always supposed to be doormats? And if so, how do we equate this text, with the numerous occasions when Jesus and Paul defended themselves and verbally attacked their accusers? These are some of the controversial issues we must take into consideration, if we want to apply this statement properly. But all is not lost beloved, for there are five key elements, which will help you to understand and apply what Peter is saying; even though it might be hard for you to apply these elements in every situation:

The act for submission is one in which we are under authority. Remember Peter addresses his statement to "servants." The word refers to household servants, but these were not just domestic employees; they were slaves. They belonged as property to their owners. So immediately, our sense of justice cries out: "But that's not fair! Slavery is evil! Slave owners are cruel! And slaves shouldn't have to submit to unjust authority! They should revolt!" But the truth is beloved, that this type of approach, just isn't the biblical way of righting the social evil of slavery. The biblical approach actually was to encourage slave owners to treat their slaves with dignity and fairness. They were even encouraged to view them as brothers and sisters in the faith (e.g., Philemon).

And slaves were exhorted to be good, submissive workers. And if they had an opportunity to gain their freedom, then all well and good. (1 Cor. 7:21). Otherwise, they were to be good slaves, in submission to their owners. So, I think we can agree, this advice did not rid the world of the evils of slavery; nor did it result in a slave revolt, although eventually slavery was eradicated.

But in the meanwhile, it did demonstrate Christlikeness within the existing social structure, in a way that led to the spread of the gospel. So beloved, how then do we apply this to our own situations, for instance, if we have to deal with an unjust boss on a regular basis? Well, we are not slaves to our employers, although we may feel like it at times. So, is it wrong to defend ourselves and to stand up for our rights, when they are violated by an employer?

Beloved, God's way is for us not to challenge authority and for us to identify the nature of the relationship we have with our bosses. Ask yourself, "Am I under the authority of the person who is treating me unfairly?" That is the first question you must ask yourself to determine how you should act in a given situation. For God has ordained various spheres of authority. He is the supreme authority overall, of course. But under God there is the sphere of human government (1 Pet. 2:13-17; Rom. 13:1-7).

Also, there is the sphere of the family, in which husbands have authority over wives (1 Pet. 3:1-6; Eph. 5:22-24) and parents over children (Eph. 6:1-4). There is the sphere of the church, in which elders have authority over the flock (1 Pet. 5:1-5; Heb. 13:17).

And there is the sphere of employment (either forced, as in slavery, or voluntary), in which employees must be subject to employers (1 Pet. 2:18; Eph. 6:5-9). Once we've identified whether or not we are under the authority of that person, beloved; who is mistreating us, then we must examine our own attitudes and motives and ask: "Do I have a proper attitude of submission, or am I selfishly fighting for my rights?" And beloved, if you are truly in submission, and are not acting out of selfish reasons, then I would agree that there is a proper place for respectful communication that seeks to clarify falsehood and promote the truth. In other words, if your attitude and motives are in submission to God; then you need not always silently endure unjust treatment, as Christian doormats. Beloved, there is a proper place for self-defence and for confronting the errors of those who have mistreated us, as long as, we work through proper channels. I make this point; because many people take the overly very erroneous view, that Christians must always "suffer in silence" and that self-defence is always wrong. But Jesus Himself did not do this, nor did the Apostle Paul, who wrote under the inspiration of the Holy Spirit.

A good example, in (John 8), speaks about 'the Jews attacking Jesus's character and authority by saying that He was bearing false witness about Himself and that He was illegitimately born.' Beloved, Jesus did not silently endure this attack. In fact, He boldly defended Himself as being sent from the Father, and He attacked His critics by saying: 'that they were of their father, the devil!' So beloved, that means that Jesus definitely did not "suffer in silence," on this occasion; nor was Jesus passive, when He attacked the Pharisees for their hypocrisy, as is spoken about in (Matthew 23).

In addition, the Apostle Paul wrote 2 Corinthians, Galatians, and parts of other epistles, to defend his character and ministry; which were often under attack. And in doing so, He derided his critics, and spoke to them in a strong and at times, a sarcastic manner. So, how can we equate such fiery, self-defence with Peter's exhortation to silent submission? Well beloved, the facts are, that every situation is different, and you must follow the leading of the Holy Spirit and align your behaviour with the Word of God, at all times concerning them. However, there are several factors to consider in deciding whether to defend yourself or indeed silently bear a reproach. First of all, 'Are you under the authority of the one attacking you?' 'And if so, you may need to examine your life to see if you are doing something to provoke the attack.' Also, then you may need to alter your behaviour entirely. In fact, you may need to even ask the person to help you with a blind spot. And in doing so, you may need to explain your motivation, as to why you took a certain action. Alternatively, if you conclude that your superior is simply out to get you, because of your faith, then you probably will need to bear the unfair treatment patiently for Christ's sake.

A second question may be: "Is God's truth being called into question or ridiculed?" If so, you should most definitely defend the truth. A good example to note, is that 'during Jesus' mockery of a trial, before the Sanhedrin, remember, He was silent until the high priest said, "I adjure You by the Living God, that You tell us whether You are the Christ, the Son of God.' 'Jesus couldn't remain silent to that question, so He answered, "You have said it yourself; nevertheless, I tell you, hereafter, you shall see the Son of Man sitting at the right hand of Power, and coming on the clouds of heaven" (Matt. 26:63-64). A third factor concerns your witness to outsiders. Beloved, if you are being falsely attacked on the job, you need to ask yourself, how you can bear the most effective witness for Jesus Christ. It may be that a quiet, but confident answer would be most effective. But, if they've heard where you stand, it may be that quiet submission, where you let go of your rights, would be most effective.

Beloved, the main thread to all of this is: 'Are you under the authority of the person who is acting unfairly towards you?' 'And if you are, then can you appeal to them with the proper attitude of submission.' But if the appeal fails, you must submit, regardless. So, does that mean that you must remain under unjust authority and tyranny for the rest of your life? And isn't there a place for getting out from under corrupt authority? The answer is, "Yes, of course; but please be careful!" For there is a place and time for Christians to flee from a corrupt government or corrupt spiritual authority, (as in the Reformation). And there is also a time for moving from a bad employer. However, the truth is, if you move too quickly, then you may miss out on what God is seeking to do in your very difficult situation. For as hard as it may be to admit to yourself, He may just be trying to teach you some very, hard lessons of how to remain Christlike. Or, He may also just want you to bear witness to others; with the motive of getting them saved and bringing into His kingdom. So please beloved, weigh things up very carefully before you make a move. Because, if you are exhibiting defiance or indeed impulsiveness, then you probably should stay exactly where you are and learn to submit. Ouch!

So, you might ask, what can I possibly gain from being submissive? Beloved, the motives for submission are to please God and to bear witness to the lost. When Peter says, "Servants, be submissive to your masters with all respect," it should be translated, "with all fear." for in the previous verse, Peter distinguished between fearing God and honouring the king. And so, when he says that we should be submissive with all fear, he means, "fear towards God," not "fear towards your earthly master."

One way to apply this beloved, is to consciously recognize, that you don't work primarily for your employer; but you work for God. I love the story that Howard Hendricks tells about being on an airliner, once; that was delayed from taking off from the airport.

For during that time, passengers grew increasingly impatient. And one very, obnoxious man kept venting his frustrations out upon the flight attendant. But she responded graciously and politely despite his unending rudeness towards her. Finally, the airplane became airborne and things at last seemed to calm down; and Dr. Hendricks called the woman over and said, "May I have your name, so that I can write a letter of commendation to your employer, for young lady you were great with that guy?" The young lady paused and smiled, and he was surprised when she replied, "Thank you, Sir, but I don't work for American Airlines." He sputtered, "You don't?" "No," she explained, "I work for my Lord Jesus Christ." She then went on to further explain, that before each flight, she and her husband would pray together that she would be a good representative of Jesus Christ on her job; and that she always sought to please God first. Beloved, Jesus Christ, suffered on our behalf and through His unjust suffering and His self-control and submission to His fate; we have been given eternal life. You see, the very concept of "self-control" implies a battle between a divided self. It implies that our "self" produces desires we should not satisfy; but instead "control." This means that we should deny ourselves and take up our cross daily and follow Jesus, as is written in (Luke 9:23). The attitude of 'fighting for our rights,' communicates to the world just the opposite, in fact; and shows that we are living for the things of this world. Beloved, submitting to unfair treatment and giving up our rights, communicates the truth that we are living as pilgrims on our way to heaven.

And truly, if you are being treated unfairly at work, you may be looking at a tremendous opportunity to bear witness for Christ by your behaviour. For if you yield your rights in a Christlike manner, people will notice and may wonder, "Why doesn't he or she fight for his rights?" Maybe you'll get an opportunity to tell them. And if so, your words are then backed up by the powerful testimony of your good works. You have then effectively demonstrated what it means to live under God's authority, with a view to pleasing Him.

Beloved, the principle of submission also involves not retaliating when we are wronged. When Jesus was wronged, when He was being cruelly nailed to the cross, He did not retaliate, for in truth; He could have called legions of angels to strike down His enemies. But He didn't. He acted selflessly, And beloved, even though we will never be as unselfish as Jesus, it is a goal we should at least, strive for. In thinking about the act of submission, let us remember Jesus's living example, as follows:

First, Jesus did not commit sin. He always acted in obedience to the Father, never in self-will. Second, there was never any deceit in His mouth. He didn't bend the facts to win the argument or get His own way. When He defended Himself, He was always truthful. Third, when He was reviled, He didn't revile in return. He didn't trade insults. Fourth, He uttered no threats. He didn't say, "Just you wait! I'll get even with you!" In other words, Jesus didn't respond to verbal abuse with more verbal abuse. Neither should we. Vengeance is always wrong for a Christian (Rom. 12:19).

Beloved, the true means of submission is to entrust ourselves to the Righteous Judge. Jesus, our Precious Saviour, made it through to the cross by continually entrusting Himself to the Father, who judges righteously. Because He knew that He would be vindicated by being raised from the dead and enthroned at the right hand of God, the Father, upon High. He also knew that His persecutors would be judged and dealt with according to their sins. And so beloved, He "delivered Himself up" to God, fully trusting in Him.

Bill Gothard tells the story of a Christian boy, who had a hostile, unbelieving father. The boy asked if he could attend the church prayer meeting one evening and the father reluctantly gave permission. As the boy walked home after the prayer meeting, a friend saw him and offered him a lift in his car. The father saw his son get out of the friend's car and said, "You lied to me about going to the prayer meeting! You really went out with your friends. Now, I'm going to punish you for that!" The boy replied, "No, I went to the prayer meeting." The father exploded, "I'm going to give you a double punishment for lying about it."

The boy quietly endured the punishment and didn't grow bitter towards his father. He loved his Dad and wanted to see him give his life to Christ. A few days later, the father was in the hardware store and ran into the Pastor of the church where his son attended. Not knowing about the punishment, the Pastor said, "You sure have a fine son. Last week in prayer meeting, he blessed us all with a fine word of testimony." The father asked, "Was my boy in the prayer meeting last week? I thought he went out with his friends." The father was broken and soon after that, he came to Christ.

Beloved, the great goal of the Christian life should be to be like Jesus. That sounds wonderful until we realize that being like Jesus means submitting to proper authority, even if it's unjust. It also means changing our attitudes and behaviour in such a way, that they please God and, so that they allow us to bear witness to the lost. It also means following Christ's example, even as He went to the cross. And it means, not retaliating; when we're wronged. It means entrusting ourselves to the Righteous Judge, beloved; knowing that someday He will right all the wrongs that have been done to us.

These are not easy things for any of us to apply. But consider the rebellious spirit of our age and of our country and ask yourself, 'If I am behaving properly towards those in authority over me, especially at work, and I am putting my whole trust in God, then won't He protect me in these situations." The Word of God promises He will protect and watch over us, beloved; in numerous places throughout the bible. I particularly love the scripture verse in (Isaiah 41:10), which says: 'So do not fear, for I am with you; do not be dismayed, for I am your God. I will strengthen you and help you; I will uphold you with my righteous right hand.'

Whilst It's true, beloved: that life isn't fair! Thank God, that Jesus Christ endured unfair treatment on our behalf, by bearing our sins upon the cross. And in so doing, He enabled us to gain eternal life! And just knowing this truth beloved, can help you to walk through any trials that may come your way. and to become more Christlike afterwards. Remember beloved, God truly is in control. Hallelujah!

# Chapter 25

## The Unstoppable Power of Decrees and Declarations

It never ceases to amaze me; how many Christians feel that once they are saved, that they can then just sit back and allow the enemy to pummel them with his attacks again and again. But beloved, having been one that has been attacked by a fair amount of the devil's tactics throughout my lifetime. I can tell you that such malaise just sets us up for a lifetime of suffering. For although God has provided us with ample tools of protection, we must not then just remain dormant; believing that God is at work without our cooperation in helping to bring that work to pass. So, let us examine what these two actions mean to start with:

-A decree is an official order issued by a legal authority. Beloved we have this authority through the name of Jesus Christ to issue these orders.
-A declaration is a formal or explicit statement or announcement.

Some might quite reasonably say, that God is able to deliver us from all evil, and to this my friend, I would wholeheartedly agree; but without us doing our part in declaring His Word and standing up against the enemy by exercising our faith through prayer and praise, our success rate in overcoming the enemy is quite diminished indeed. And one such way to ensure we are overcomers and not sufferers during our lives is by utilising decrees or declarations.

Beloved, the truth is, the entire universe is waiting for us to give it instruction. And the Bible speaks about this in (Romans 8:19): "For the earnest expectation of the creation eagerly waits for the revealing of the sons of God" What this means beloved, is that the whole universe waits in anticipation for the sons and daughters of God to manifest themselves; and bring it back into alignment with God's original intent for them. Hallelujah!

And God demonstrated this Himself, as is referred to in (Hebrews 11:3): "the universe was created by the Word of God, so that what is seen was not made out of things that are visible." In fact, in the book of Genesis, Chapter One, at the beginning of each day of the creation story, we see this principle being carried out by the declaration: "And God said, 'Let there be...'" You see beloved, God spoke out what He had seen in His mind, and then He spoke, the earth, all the planets, the sun, moon, and stars, as well as every plant, animal, and human being into existence.

James, the brother of Jesus, also told a parable of how this "declaration principle" is to work in our lives and said: "For we all stumble in many ways. And if anyone does not stumble in what he says, he is a perfect man, able also to bridle his whole body. If we put bits into the mouths of horses so that they obey us, we guide their whole bodies, as well.

Look at the ships also: though they are so large and are driven by strong winds, they are guided by a very small rudder wherever the will of the pilot directs. So also, the tongue is a small member, yet it boasts of great things, (James 3:2-5).

Beloved, it is very important that you take the time necessary to carefully consider your course in life. For where you are headed and what it will look like when you get there, at least in the broad sense, forms and shapes a reality for you to speak into and declare over, until it actually does come into existence. And don't let anyone take that dream or vision away from you by their negative words or unbelief. For there is nothing wrong with having a vision, as long as, it lines up with God's will and purpose for your life. So often, I have seen people become double minded in regards to their dream or vision; because they start to align themselves with the negativity and unbelief that has been foisted upon them; and before you know it, that dream or vision is stalled, if not cancelled altogether, which is certainly Satan's master plan.

In (James 1:8), it says: "A double minded man is unstable in all of his ways." In addition, such double mindedness can occur because of impatience on our own parts, and when we get tired of waiting for our vision to be fulfilled, we then start complaining and get into a place of disobedience with God. Believe me, beloved, I have learned this the hard way, that this type of behaviour just slows things down, and causes huge obstruction to the vision that we initially wanted to speed up in the first place. Remember, that your every decree holds both the power and potential to transform your life? This truth is evident in (Psalm 2:7-8), which says: "I will proclaim the Lord's decree:

He said to me, "You are my son; today I have become your father. Ask me, and I will make the nations your inheritance, and the ends of the earth your possession." Hallelujah!

Here are some wonderful examples of powerful declarations that have worked in my own life and I am sure it will in yours too, if you use them with the right heart:

- I AM complete in Him Who is the Head of all principalities and powers (Colossians 2:10).

- I AM alive with Christ (Ephesians 2:5).

- I AM free from the law of sin and death (Romans 8:2).

- I AM far from oppression, and fear does not come near me (Isaiah 54:14).

- I AM born of God, and the evil one does not touch me (1 John 5:18).

- I AM holy and without blame before Him in love (Ephesians 1:4; 1 Peter 1:16).

- I have the mind of Christ (1 Corinthians 2:16; Philippians 2:5).

- I have the peace of God that surpasses all understanding (Philippians 4:7).

- I have the Greater One living in me; greater is He Who is in me than he who is in the world (1 John 4:4).

- I have received the spirit of wisdom and revelation in the knowledge of Jesus, the eyes of my understanding being enlightened (Ephesians 1:17, 18).

**Building Cleansing Declaration:**

Dear Heavenly Father,
You are God of Heaven and Earth and there is no one like You. We acknowledge the Lordship of Jesus Christ, in our lives and over this building. By Your Sovereign Plan, You, have entrusted to us many things. Thank you for this building Lord. We claim this building, as a place of spiritual safety for all who enter here, and we commit to living by faith and promoting Your purposes, Father God, in this place. Lord. we ask You to come and make Your abode here in this building, thus making it safe from all the attacks of the enemy. For Satan doesn't intimidate You, therefore, he doesn't intimidate us. As Your children. Father God, we receive the truth that You raised us up and seated us in heavenly places in Christ Jesus. This is our position.

Therefore, and as a result of our position: in the Name of The Lord Jesus Christ, we command every evil spirit, who claims ground in this place, based on the activities of past or present or nearby occupiers, including ourselves and our loved ones, to LEAVE and NEVER RETURN. GET OUT NOW. We bind up any and all demonic strategies assigned to this place.

Father God, and we ask You to post your angels around this building to guard it from all attempts of the enemy to enter and disturb us or anyone who enters this building. We make these requests and declarations in the Name of Jesus, who has all authority over the heavens, the earth, and under the earth. And now I simply rest in Your Love My Heavenly Father. And we give You Praise, Amen.

# Chapter 26

## A Heart of Giving

My friend, as Christians, we are the light of the world, as it says in (Matthew 5:14-16), "You are the light of the world. A town built on a hill cannot be hidden. Neither do people light a lamp and put it under a bowl. Instead, they put it on its' stand, and it gives light to everyone in the house. In the same way, let your light shine before others, that they may see your good deeds and glorify your Father in heaven. Now beloved, most of us have heard the mentality, in the Christian World; which says: "If we sow in, we will get back," and usually it is said, in reference to our money." And I am not denying that there is a biblical principle and even a command in reference to our tithes and offerings in the Word of God. But truly beloved, I don't believe the act of giving is so one dimensional. For having a heart of giving, encompasses a pathway to ministry so immense, that very few people have understood its' true magnitude before. So, let us examine a very important part of this scripture, in verse 16; which says, "when people (the unsaved), see our good deeds, that it will glorify our Father in Heaven." Beloved, this verse is talking about our actions done in mercy and compassion for the lost, the impoverished and the broken hearted. Now this may mean by using money and it may not, for there are plenty of Christian wives out there, that cannot give a tithe or offering for that matter; because of the restrictions placed upon them by their unsaved our unenlightened spouses, yet, they give of themselves selflessly to do any number of things to help those less fortunate. Well, you might say then, "but Leisa this just sounds like charity work and not ministry at all." But the simple truth is, it becomes ministry when it "Glorifies God."

So, what does it mean to glorify God? Beloved, to glorify God, means we bring Him honour through what we say, how we act, and how we think. To glorify God means to acknowledge His glory and to value it above all things. It also means we make it known to others; and it means we have a heartfelt gratitude for all the things God has done for us. We glorify God through our faith, through our love and through our desire to obey Him. And mostly we glorify God through our desire to know Him and to be His child. And as we become more and more who God has called us to be – more like Him – through the process of cleansing and sanctification, we reflect God more and more. We then become more loving, more gracious, and, yes, more giving. Because God is generous, we are also called to be generous. Generosity beloved, not only points others to God; but it is an appropriate response to what God has done for us and also, gives us authority in the 'Courts of Heaven,' when we make petitions in prayer, as our sacrifice is recognised and is acceptable to God. So, how can we walk endued by God's power with a true heart of giving towards others?

Well, several scriptures hold the key to this wonderful journey, such as, (Luke 12:48), which summarises: 'Because we have been so freely loved, we now freely love others,' and (John 13:34), which summarises: 'Because we have been forgiven, we forgive others,' And in (Matthew 18:21-25), which summarises: 'Our response to God's abundance with us, is to share that abundance with others. And when we then receive God's overwhelming generosity, it humbles us. We then recognize that we are not worthy of His gift at all. Out of gratefulness, we then become more gracious with others; as we begin to learn about the wonderful, loving heart of God and want to be more like Him."

Generosity definitely does have positive and even life changing effects upon human relationships. In fact, when one person gives freely to another, then quite often the recipient often "passes on" the gift to someone else in need. And beloved, in the Christian life, this represents an absolute bedrock of our faith, as Jesus taught us that "it is more blessed to give than to receive" as is written about in (Acts 20:35). For if we truly want to be the personification of God on earth demonstrating His very character to the unsaved, then we must be willing to give of our time, our talents, our mercy, our compassion, our giftings, and yes, our possessions and money, as the Holy Spirit directs. You see beloved, God wants us to be His vessels in this life, full of the Holy Spirit and ready to do whatever He asks of us, as His children, to bring in the harvest of unsaved souls into His kingdom. William Shakespeare wrote about "the quality of mercy." Which seems a very able phrase to me. For as Christians we must examine our motives for being generous and giving to others.

He writes:
The quality of mercy is not strain'd,
It droppeth as the gentle rain from heaven

Upon the place beneath: it is twice blest;
It blesseth him that gives and him that takes:
Tis mightiest in the mightiest: it becomes
The throned monarch better than his crown;
His sceptre shows the force of temporal power,
The attribute to awe and majesty,
Wherein doth sit the dread and fear of kings;
But mercy is above this sceptred sway;
It is enthroned in the hearts of kings,
It is an attribute to God himself;

Beloved, to be like Him in your words, deeds, and actions; is to have a true heart of giving, and will make you whole, as you walk in the purposes of God. It amazes me that so many Christians are so uncertain of what they should be doing in reference to "their ministry or their destiny." And many wait for absolute years, just hoping and praying for a Word from God to lead them in the right direction. Trust me, my friend, if you start showing generosity, mercy and compassion towards others and you walk led of the Holy Spirit, you will not only know your ministry and destiny in God, you will be running to keep up with all the blessings and opportunities God will put your way, Hallelujah!

# Chapter 27

## Prayer Solutions for Barren Women

Beloved, as a minister that God uses to bring about healing to those in need, I have come upon many barren women that are barren because the enemy has attached to them, through an 'Accuser of the Brethren' Spirit, and this spirit is described in (Revelations 12:10), which says: "Then I heard a loud voice in heaven say: "Now have come the salvation and the power, and the kingdom of our God, and the authority of His Messiah. For the accuser of our brothers and sisters, who accuses them before our God day and night, has been hurled down." Beloved, the "Accuser of the Brethren" Spirit is a savage spirit that attacks a person's self-worth day and night. This accusing and spiteful spirit is an anti-Christ spirit, because it approaches people with a loveless tone of condemnation and shame. This vile spirit works through a voice of never-ending condemnation, and constantly tells a person how much of a failure they are, by pointing out their weaknesses to convince people of their unworthiness. This is in fact, the polar-opposite nature of God; as it tears down people rather than building them up. The Spirit is very legalistic and uses the bible oftentimes, to lay heavy burdens and crush its' victims, just as the Pharisees did to Jesus. There are many barren women in the bible: Hannah, Sarah, Rebekah, Rachel, and Elisabeth; and each of these women opened up doors, as a result of their own sin conditions, which allowed the "Accuser of the Brethren" Spirit to attach to their soul realms (emotions and mind); which caused them to suffer some degree of torment until they achieved their breakthrough from God.

One such woman was Hannah, the Prophet Samuel's mother. Her story is in 1 Samuel, Chapters one and two, and it describes how her husband Elkanah, had two wives, which was a major source of conflict within his family. For although in Old Testament times God tolerated polygamy, the bible never really portrays in in a good light. In fact, God's original plan has always been for one man and one woman to be in a committed marriage for life. And any violation of this plan, whether it is several wives at the same time, or a succession of wives (or husbands), due to divorce, can create problems.

In Elkanah's family life, the tension was increased disproportionately; because one of his wives, Penninah, had many children (a clear sign of God's blessing in that time era), while the other wife, Hannah, had none at all. And to complicate matters even worse, Elkanah favoured Hannah, over Penninah, which caused immense jealousy between the two women. This led of course, to ongoing rivalry between the two women. For instance, when they went to worship at the tabernacle, as they did faithfully each year; at the appointed time, Elkanah tried to balance the rivalry between the women by giving double portions of food to Hannah, who was the wife without children, instead of Penninah, which did not go down well, I can assure you. In fact, his actions made the situation between the women infinitely worse, because Peninnah would then constantly say to Hannah, "You've got the food, but I've got the children!" Hannah would then cry and Elkanah would wring his hands and try to comfort her by saying, "Am I not better to you than ten sons?" And in (1 Samuel Chapter 1:8): Hannah because she was feeling shamed and of low self-worth, would not answer that question! For as she listened to the "Accuser of the Brethren" Spirit; all she could think about was, "Why doesn't God bless me with children? And why has He blessed this mean-spirited woman above me?"

Beloved, children are a blessing from the Lord, and motherhood is a gift to mankind, and after promising her child to God and humbling herself before Him, no doubt in repentance; she did at last, give birth to Samuel, her child. In many cultures across the ages, a woman's value has been and is based upon her ability to reproduce. Sadly, a woman's entire worth is evaluated and indeed heightened, if she gives birth to a son. And believe me, the "Accuser of the Brethren" Spirit capitalises on this state of being; as he sinks these poor women into a deep pit of despair, if they are barren and cannot have children.

Let us examine together the open doors that might be responsible for barrenness in a woman; for beloved, it is my firm belief, that any type of illness or condition that is believed to be incurable or insolvable, is in fact, caused by a demonic spirit, who has attached itself to a person in the physical realm. As stated, before in this book, this occurs because of either a generational curse or wilful disobedience on the part of the person with the condition.

Now beloved, I do not believe that anyone should be heaped upon with more condemnation, when they are ill, or have ongoing health issues: because some sin conditions are pretty complex and are formed and shaped in such a way, that this behaviour is part of a person's identity, which takes time to overcome.

But I do want people afflicted with barrenness or incurable disease; to understand the root cause of such conditions; so that they can move to a greater place of faith; and overcome their suffering, once and for all, through God's healing power. In (Genesis 11:30), it talks about Sarah, Abraham's wife; who bitterly accepted her barrenness; and had taken it on as her identity. It says: "Now Sarai was barren; she had no child." Sarah is the first woman beloved, mentioned in the bible that was barren. And interestingly, God chose her and Abraham to be the forbearers of the great nation of Israel. Now beloved, this couple seemed a very strange choice, when they were not only unable to have children; but they were also quite old. Not to mention Sarah had grown so bitter about her barrenness; that she had total unbelief in God's plans to make her a mother.

She even laughed when the angel prophesied about her upcoming pregnancy, and prior to her pregnancy she offered her servant, Hagar, to birth a son for her husband and then cruelly cast her out of the camp after she (Sarah), finally gave birth to Isaac.

The tension between the two women had become unbearable, as they vied for Abraham's attentions; for themselves and for their sons. In fact, at a celebration after Isaac was weaned, Sarah found the teenage Ishmael mocking her son, Isaac. And she was so upset by it, that she demanded that Abraham send Hagar and her son away, for good. And Sarah further, boldly declared; that Ishmael would not share in Isaac's inheritance. Abraham was greatly distressed by the situation; but God told Abraham to do as his wife commanded, because His plan would be carried out through both Isaac and Ishmael, regardless of the situation; and so, Abraham did as God commanded. What this means beloved is, that in spite of Sarah's sin condition of jealousy, anger, bitterness, and unbelief; God made the impossible, possible; because of Abraham's faithfulness,

Beloved, God desires for us to live long and prosper in all our ways. In (Psalm 113:9), it says: "He gives the barren woman a home, making her the joyous mother of children." Praise the Lord!" I can remember one meeting I attended of which, I was not the main speaker; and at the time, I was sitting in a chair on the stage of the church after just having led the worship, and my husband was meant to minister the Word of God that day. The church he had been asked to speak at, was in West Texas, and it was filled to the brim with both visitors and church members. And as I sat quietly, I suddenly looked to my right and there seated beside me, was none other than the Lord Jesus Christ; and He told me 'that He wanted me to speak a Word of Knowledge to a woman of whom He loved very much in the meeting, and that if I was obedient then He would open her womb and she would be able to bear a child." Well, I started to give excuses trying to explain to the Lord, that it was 'not my meeting,' and then I looked at Him again and saw the compassion in His eyes, as He pointed to the front. Well that was enough for me, and before I knew it, I was on my feet to inform my husband what the Lord had directed me to do, which he submitted to immediately, as he had the witness of the Holy Spirit.

Well, the Word the Lord gave me was about "a barren woman who was sitting in the back of the church," and He said to tell her over the microphone in the front of that church, "that if she would just overcome her shame and embarrassment, and believe in faith, that He could open her womb, and that He would grant her a miracle that very day."

Now beloved, I don't mind telling you I stood for a full five minutes, before anyone even moved in that church, And I was to the point, that I would need to overcome my own embarrassment too, if something didn't happen soon. But after the five minutes elapsed, suddenly a very tall man on the right hand side of the church; jumped up and shouted, "The Lord says, this is a prophetess of the Most High God and if you are obedient, church; then He will grant you many miracles this day." I learned later that this man was an elder of the church, and directly after he loudly prophesied that Word of the Lord, I heard a woman scream from the back of the church, and she came running up to the front to get prayer, and it was the very woman who needed to be set free from her barrenness. I, then immediately prayed for her, and she said she felt a warmth enter her lower abdomen region; as God performed His miracle. This woman's faith, beloved, not only brought her miracle into a place of reality; but encouraged others of whom God wanted to heal that day. Gloriously, I saw a deaf man receive his hearing, and broken limbs healed during that service, as God rained down His healing touch upon those blessed people. And exactly ten months later, I received a letter from the Pastor of that church and glory hallelujah that supposedly barren women had given birth to a lovely, baby girl. That dear woman had chosen to lay aside her shame and acceptance of a false identity, the enemy had labelled her with; as a "barren woman." And just believed God to change everything in a matter of minutes and He did. Praise God!

# Chapter 28

## The Real Deal About Marriage and Love Relationships

The concept of love and marriage from a worldly perspective has been remarkably distorted in the modern-day world. You see, beloved, Satan's master plan is to deeply embed the practice of idolatry to self upon mankind. This practice thoroughly disturbs the equilibrium of Christians and Non-Christians alike; as they are inundated with films, music, television and the worldwide web supporting this concept. In addition, it is critically important to remember that Satan uses these things to influence our body and soul (mind and emotions) realms, so completely; that the spiritual realm is ignored; and then terrible darkness and afflictions occur, such as broken relationships, divorce, jealousy, suicide and sexual immorality. Such sin conditions cause doors to fly wide open, and then demonic attachments can follow like: mental illness, murder, and infirmity, just to name a few.

Beloved, as Christians, we must approach marriage and love relationships from an entirely different angle, bearing in mind that we are created in God's image; and He desires for us to be aligned and balanced in these relationships, God knows that we need our emotional and physical needs met in our marriage relationships; but He also requires us to put in the effort, so that we are as spiritually aligned as possible with our partners, or we will end up being unequally yoked; and often, this requires, patience, love and a lot of prayer. So, let us explore what God's word says about being unequally yoked. (2 Corinthians 6:14), says: "Do not be unequally yoked with unbelievers. For what partnership has righteousness with lawlessness? Or what fellowship has light with darkness?" It also says in (1 Corinthians 7:12-15): "To the rest I say that if any brother has a wife who is an unbeliever, and she consents to live with him, he should not divorce her. If any woman has a husband who is an unbeliever, and he consents to live with her, she should not divorce him. For the unbelieving husband is made holy because of his wife, and the unbelieving wife is made holy because of her husband. Otherwise, your children would be unclean, but as it is, they are holy. But if the unbelieving partner separates, let it be so. In such cases the brother or sister is not enslaved. God has called you to peace." These scriptures beloved, are very important, because they give us insight about how important it is to God, that there is peace, unity and alignment in our marriages. In the case of love relationships, leading up to marriage; the spiritual alignment of a couple must be the most important goal to achieve, as they walk together in unity, honouring God. The second goal must be to become aligned in the soul realm, so that there is adequate understanding between the couple, regarding each other's emotions and thought processes. Of course, this is infinitely easier, if they are spiritually aligned, and understand how important it is to walk in the fruits of the spirit, so that they treat each other with love and respect, at all times.

Beloved, I am not in any way saying that the third part, our bodies, or (the physical realm) is not important or should not be in alignment, between the couple, for I believe it is. But I also know that if the first two realms are developed and are firmly aligned, then the physical realm between the couple will quite naturally reach its' desired outcome. This is so, because the physical realm is so entirely dependent on the other two realms, that if the couple only base their commitment on their attraction and physical love, that they have for each other, then their relationship will eventually break down.

In all my years of counselling Christians, I have found that must marital breakdowns are due to the spirit, soul and body being misaligned. In fact, many marriages only focus on one part of the alignment; which is the physical, and the husband or wife's emotional needs or ignored altogether, And maybe one partner in the relationship is following after God in their spiritual walk; but they have so badly judged their partner; because of the emotional neglect that he or she has heaped upon them, that they no longer want to reach out to them to come into line with them spiritually or emotionally, at all. Sadly, then after some time, even the partner who was trying to serve God gets so discouraged, that they too falter, and there inevitably is a total disconnect of any alignment whatsoever, between the body, soul, and spirit of the couple and the marriage breaks down.

Beloved, we must cherish our marriage relationships, because in the Bible, God speaks phrases in His Word like "hold fast to his wife" and "they shall become one flesh;" which clearly support the premise, that there is something much deeper and more permanent that should be considered, rather than engaging in serial marriages and occasional adultery. In fact, what these words actually point out, is the fact, that marriage is a sacred covenant, which should be a rooted and grounded commitment, that stands against every storm for "as long as they both shall live."

But these phrases only imply this, and it becomes much more transparent, when the mystery of marriage is examined in fuller revelation in the passage, (Ephesians 5:31–32), when Paul quotes from (Genesis 2:24), and in verse 31, where he says: "'Therefore a man shall leave his father and mother and hold fast to his wife, and the two shall become one flesh.'" And then Paul gives his all-important interpretation of this scripture in verse 32, and says: "This mystery is profound, and I am saying that it refers to Christ and the church." In other words, marriage beloved, is patterned after Christ's covenant commitment to His church. You see, Christ thought of himself as the bridegroom coming for his bride (the church), the true people of God. And Paul knew his ministry was to gather the bride, the true people of God; who would trust Christ. He further says, in (2 Corinthians 11:2): "I feel a divine jealousy for you, since I betrothed you to one husband, to present you (the church), as a pure virgin to Christ."

Beloved, Jesus Christ knew He would have to pay the dowry of His own blood for His redeemed bride. In fact, He called this relationship, the new covenant, in (Luke 22:20), which says: "This cup that is poured out for you is the new covenant in my blood." And clearly beloved, this is what Paul is referring to, when he speaks about marriage being a great mystery, for he is comparing marriage between a man and a woman, to Jesus Christ, and the new covenant church, (or his bride); and saying it is a Holy bond. In fact, with marriage relationships being patterned after Jesus Christ and the new covenant church, we can say without question, that marriage exists for God's glory. That is, it exists to display God, and has purpose in it. For beloved, if we are aligned as a couple, in body, soul, and spirit, then we are in effect as God's Word says: "two or more gathered together in His name." which is spoken about inn (Matthew 18:20), where God promises "He is with us."

Now I know after reading such words, some of you, who have experienced broken relationships and divorce; may hear the enemy whispering words to you, that "you are a failure." But beloved remember "there is no condemnation in Christ Jesus," as is written in (Romans 8:1); and I know God is the great restorer and healer of our wounds, as is written in (Jeremiah 30:17). So, I would encourage you to learn from your experiences, and start seeking to become aligned in all ways to God's purposes for your life. And I pray, that great understanding has been grounded in your spirits, of how to have strong, healthy, Godly relationships in the future, Amen.

# Chapter 29

## The Winds of Transition

Beloved, as you go through the process of changing to align yourself with God's purposes, you will experience a paradigm shift in every area of your life, as God refines you, which is confirmed in (Malachi 3:3): "He will sit as a refiner and purifier of silver; He will purify the Levites (His church); and refine them like gold and silver. Then the LORD will have men, who will bring offerings in righteousness," it is important during this special time, as God blows the winds of transition your way, that you consider any talents or abilities you may have developed and been successful with, in the past, which will assist you in your glorious future of serving God. For the truth is, we are in the latter days, beloved; and I believe God is equipping His people at a much faster pace. And remember, that God can build upon your past experiences, so it is important to make sure that you are positioned to allow your past to be of benefit to the Kingdom of God. Believe me, beloved, your involvement and experiences whether in ministry, or education, in social settings, or in a professional capacity; are all valuable and have been training ground for what God has been preparing you for in the future. And oddly, even past experiences that you might have deemed as total failures; can prepare you in a very unique way.

This occurs, by enabling you to identify and help people that are going through the same issues that you did. Beloved, remember that we are all broken vessels that must ask for God's forgiveness, strength and help each and every day. And so, don't find it strange when God starts using you to progress His kingdom, before you feel like you are actually ready. With this in mind, it is important to remember that it is God who is working through you to make a difference in people's lives. And as long as you love Him with all of your heart and are trying to live and walk in His righteousness and strength, then God will gradually use you more and more. In fact, when God does start using you, He will start to shift you from one assignment to another, and you will go through a process of preparation, like you have never known before. And through these assignments, beloved, you will have more and more of what I like to call "rhema moments." These moments occur as God leads and guides you through the presence of the Holy Spirit in your life.

Fascinatingly, the definition of rhema is 'a verse or portion of Scripture that the Holy Spirit brings to our attention with application to a current situation or need for direction.' And the good news is, there is so much power as you speak or act upon a 'rhema moment' and are led by the Holy Spirit, that the breakthroughs you will witness will be mind-blowing. This is the kind of power, beloved, that most people only dream about, and this makes serving God a wonderful adventure. For through this preparation time, He is teaching you how to hear His voice; and also, how to move in the fullness of His Spirit. And beloved, as you sense Him leading you to the next level, you will begin to discern specifics about the next assignment about to take place. This type of prophetic preparation is not necessarily based on your past; but must take place, in the "here and now" and more than likely, will involve the practical changes you need to make in your life, in order to actually fulfil the new assignment God has in mind for you.

Many times, people think they will be prepared for a new assignment, if they just pray more, worship more and read the Bible more regularly. But the truth is, that each person and assignment is unique and different. And only the manifold wisdom of God can truly determine what changes are actually necessary. These disciplines are important in times of transition, but there are also natural components to the changes God will bring in your life; as He moves you forward. Be ready beloved, for moving into that new level or season, will impact every area of your life, in one way or another. It is also important, as God's servant, to commit to overcoming the opposition. For very often, when God begins to move you to the next level, you will encounter various forms of opposition. And as He moves you forward, the devil wants to move you backward, or at least to cause you to stay right where you are. In fact, the enemy will do everything possible to flood you with thoughts and emotions that are counterproductive to God's purposes in your life. But this is the time to stand and resist Satan and He will have to flee, and it may take a week, a month or even a year; but God's Word promises this, in (James 4:7). Do not expect your transition into God's purposes for your life, to be easy, beloved; but I can say from experience, that when you have overcome the mountain that stands between you and the destiny that God has called you into, that the feeling of fulfilment burns so deeply within the inner core of your spirit, that you truly will understand what the Prophet Jeremiah was talking about, in Chapter 20, verse 9: when he said, "His Word is in my heart and is like a fire, a fire shut up in my bones. I am weary of holding it in; indeed, I cannot."

Beloved, God requires us to be flexible and not to be too set in our ways; for He will move us out of our comfort zones; and truly stretch us, challenge us and bombard us; with a plethora of new experiences that are frankly unfamiliar and even a bit intimidating at times. So much so, that sometimes you can't believe that God has actually chosen, "little old you," to work through, to perform that miracle, or perform that healing, or lead that youth group full of rowdy teenagers, or to go into that prison ministry, or any number of unusual ministry options, you did not previously see yourself getting involved in.

One very, interesting character that experienced just these types of feelings in the Bible, when God called him into a state of transition, was a man called Gideon, who is described in (Judges, Chapters 6-8). Gideon was an unassuming, young man, whose tribe Manasseh, was the weakest of all of the tribes of Israel, and yet, God called him to deliver Israel from the Midianites. The situation was dire for the Israelites, as is described In, (Judges 6:1-8): "The Israelites did evil in the eyes of the Lord, and for seven years He gave them into the hands of the Midianites. Because the power of Midian was so oppressive, the Israelites prepared shelters for themselves in mountain clefts, caves and strongholds. Whenever the Israelites planted their crops, the Midianites, Amalekites and other eastern peoples invaded the country. They camped on the land and ruined the crops all the way to Gaza, and did not spare a living thing for Israel, neither sheep nor cattle nor donkeys.

They came up with their livestock and their tents like swarms of locusts. It was impossible to count them or their camels; they invaded the land to ravage it. Midian so impoverished the Israelites that they cried out to the Lord for help."

Beloved, Gideon was that help, despite his lack of confidence in his own abilities. And each time Gideon brought up a reason, politely to God, why He couldn't possibly, do the thing that God had called him to do, God answered him, by saying: "I will be with you." And through a dream, the Lord showed Gideon exactly what to do, and he was obedient to God's instructions, as is written in Judges 7:19-22; "Gideon and the hundred men with him reached the edge of the camp at the beginning of the middle watch, just after they had changed the guard. They blew their trumpets and broke the jars that were in their hands. The three companies blew the trumpets and smashed the jars. Grasping the torches in their left hands and holding in their right hands the trumpets they were to blow, they shouted, "A sword for the Lord and for Gideon!" While each man held his position around the camp, all the Midianites ran, crying out as they fled. When the three hundred trumpets sounded, the Lord caused the men throughout the camp to turn on each other with their swords..." Beloved, Gideon and his men then chased what was left of the enemy and drove them out of their lands, because God fulfilled His promise and was with Gideon. Hallelujah!

Be prepared for increased spiritual attacks, as you move out for the Lord. But Winston Churchill the great Primes Minister of the United Kingdom, during World War II, once said: "Success is not final, failure is not fatal: it is the courage to continue that counts." And just as Gideon had courage to fulfil

God's plan for his life, so must you and "God will be with you." Remember, the more you move into God's unfolding purposes for your life, the more effective you will become for Him—and the more of a threat you will become to the kingdom of darkness. We know that Jesus came to earth to destroy the works of the devil (see 1 John 3:8) and we know that, in Him, we are assured of victory in every situation (see 2 Cor. 2:14). But this certainty of victory does not eliminate the battle. We have an enemy; that we are engaged in a spiritual war with; and we must fight. And whilst attacks from our opposition may intensify, when we move from one level to the next; and transition into a new season or take on a new assignment, the comforting truth is, that if we use the power of God's Word to defeat Satan through prayer and get others to pray for us, then Satan and his minions, have no choice, but to flee.

Sometimes beloved, new battles may require new strategies; as directed by the Holy Spirit, but your basic weaponry remains the same. For in Christ, you have spiritual armour to protect you against the attacks of the enemy (see Eph. 6:13-18). And you also have the weapon of His Word, the power of His Spirit and the reinforcement of other believers.

# Chapter 30

## Why Repentence?

Beloved, there is a wonderful scripture in the Bible in (Revelations 3:8), which says: "I know your deeds. See, I have placed before you an open door that no one can shut. I know that you have little strength, yet you have kept My Word and have not denied My Name." This important scripture speaks of the keys of repentance and obedience and both must be in operation, before God releases a new season for us; which can contain both blessing and opportunity. The next scripture in (Revelations 3:9), goes on to talk about God's validation over our lives; as we walk in repentance and obedience, and says: "I will make those who are of the synagogue of Satan, who claim to be Jews, though they are not, but are liars--I will make them come and fall down at your feet and acknowledge that I have loved you." Beloved, this verse is telling us, "that if we are walking in obedience and repentance before the Lord; then every demonic spirit, including religious ones; will have to submit to the authority God gives us, as His children. So, you might ask the question; "but why then, do I need to keep repenting, when I have already accepted Jesus Christ as my Saviour, and He has forgiven all my sins?" This is an excellent question, so let's examine why this is important.

    First of all, beloved, repentance gives an open invitation to God to restore, forgive and purify us, as we humbly come before Him and ask for His cleansing touch. We are in effect, asking for our Father, God to reach out and help us in our sinful state. This ensures there is an intimacy between God, the Father, and ourselves, and that all of our guilt is washed away entirely; as we ask God to grant this through the Blood of Jesus. This is beautifully depicted in (Zechariah 1:3), which says: "Therefore tell the people: This is what the Lord Almighty says: 'Return to me,' declares the Lord Almighty, 'and I will return to you.'

Secondly, Repentance helps us to remain humble. Most of us have found that when we have had trouble repenting, it's often because of pride issues in our own lives. Beloved, without a doubt, pride brings about a spiritual blindness that can cause us to believe that our standards are actually better than God's standards. This is very dangerous and can cause terrible repercussions, if we do not check ourselves and renew our minds, whilst submitting to God. Humility goes hand in hand with a teachable spirit and most Christians have found (including myself); that as they walk with God on the journey of life, they never stop learning, never.

Perhaps that is why Paul says that repentance leads us to know the truth, so that we can come to our senses (2 Timothy 2:25-26). In other words, as we repent and learn to agree with the truth of God's standards of righteousness and sin, we can then begin to exhibit the basic rudiments of humility in our own behaviour, and we can grow in grace, as we learn to walk in humility more and more. You see, beloved, God values humility; and what's more He actually shows favour to those who are humble. This is shown in, (James 4:10), which says: "Humble yourselves before the Lord, and He will lift you up in honour." In contrast God opposes the proud, which is very clear in (James 4:6), and many other books in the Bible. The third reason why we should repent, is that such actions actually drive the devil away from us. Now, all of us have engaged in wilful disobedience to God, and as mentioned before in the previous chapters of this book, such actions done without genuine repentance, can indeed open up doors to demonic attack. Also, when this happens, the enemy can more easily convince us of his lies by saying things like: "God doesn't love you anymore," "You've really blown it this time." "God won't give you a second chance," and "God has given up on you now." These are all the voices of harassing spirits and can certainly gain a foothold in our minds without genuine repentance on our part. Beloved, when we sin, we're actually giving the devil permission to draw near to us. This is confirmed in, (John 8:44), which says: "You are of your father the devil, and the desires of your father you want to do. He was a murderer from the beginning, and does not stand in the truth, because there is no truth in him." "When he speaks a lie, he speaks from his own resources, for he is a liar and the father of it." But thankfully, when we repent and return to God, these deceptive whispers of the enemy will start to fade and then they will go completely in time. For when you are in right standing with God, they have no legal right to hang around, Hallelujah!

    The fourth reason why we should repent before God, is because it frees us from the torment of sin. Beloved, have you ever heard the saying: "Well, you made your bed, so now you will have to lie in it." This saying is particularly relevant, when we wilfully choose to continue living in our sinful ways and do not repent before God. For although sin may feel good at the time, it ultimately wounds us far more than we actually realise; and can scar us for life. For sin gives these tormenting spirits free license to plant guilt, addictions, infirmity, and all sorts of attachments to our bodies and souls, as we walk in an unrepentant state. With this being the case, we must be ever grateful that God gives us the opportunity to confess and repent of our sins, for this is a means for us to receive His mercy and grace. (1 Corinthians 10:13), says: "You are tempted in the same way that everyone else is tempted. But God can be trusted not to let you be tempted too much, and He will show you how to escape from your temptations."

Lastly beloved, repentance ensures a victorious and fulfilled life and destiny; as we walk in God's authority, as His children. We can then apply the blood of Jesus, as we pray and not only ask for mercy for ourselves; but also, for others, who so desperately need the saving grace of the Lord, Jesus Christ. Sin will only ultimately lead to spiritual death; and God's Word tells us plainly that "the wages of sin is death" in Romans 6:23. And Jesus himself, said, "unless you repent, you too will all perish" in (Luke 13:3).

I am happy to confirm through experiences in my own life, that when we repent, we are in effect inviting the Lord Jesus Christ, through the person of the Holy Spirit, to have fellowship with us. For after urging Christians to "be earnest and repent," Jesus said, "Here I am! I stand at the door and knock.

If anyone hears My voice and opens the door, I will come in and eat with that person, and they with Me" (Revelation 3:19-20). Beloved, we need God's mercy and grace and His ever-empowering presence, to walk through all the difficulties of life; and this can only be achieved through true repentance and obedience to the Almighty God, Amen.

# Chapter 31

## The Practical Application of Visions and Dreams

In this modern-day world that we all live in, there are many people who might have the tendency to marginalise the occurrence of dreams and visions in the life of a Christian. But it is my belief, that if we seek to hear the voice of God through the presence and person of the Holy Spirit, then we will need to be flexible with God as to how He wants to deliver a message to us. Because frankly beloved, if He was able to make a donkey talk to Balaam, the pay per view prophet, spoken about in (Numbers 22:28), then He can certainly speak through the dreams and visions of His people.

In (Joel 2:28), God promised, "I will pour out My Spirit upon all people. Your sons and daughters will prophesy. Your old men will dream dreams, and your young men will see visions." Without question, dreams and visions are two exciting and powerful ways God can speak to His children; and throughout His Word, God has used these insightful messages to give specific instruction in the areas of warnings, present and future spiritual knowledge, and for edification of the Body of Christ. Dreams and Vision interpretation has been widely discussed in Christian circles for many generations; but the truth is, that whosoever has had the dream or vision, should be able to bring the interpretation of it. For just as God imparts a prophetic word to one of His children, that they are meant to convey to the wider body of believers, and they are held responsible for its' interpretation; so too, must a dreamer or a visionary be equally responsible, for what God gives them.

Beloved there are all kinds of recipes for accurate dream or vision interpretation; but truly, if you ask God what the meaning of a dream or a vision is, He will most assuredly tell you. This is confirmed in (Psalms 84:11), where it says: "For the Lord God is a sun and shield: the Lord will give grace and glory: no good thing will he withhold from them that walk uprightly." Also, in God's Word. it says in, (1 Corinthians 14:32): "The spirits of prophets are subject to the control of prophets," Now beloved, I am not trying to say that everyone that has a dream of a vision is a prophet; but I would concede that they would most likely, have a gift of prophesy of which they are responsible for. This means that if they don't have the interpretation for either the dream or the vision, then they must press into God through prayer and perhaps fasting until the answer comes.

There is no one that can say that spiritual dreams are not biblical, for in actuality, the word "dream" appears 87 times in the Old Testament and eight times in the New Testament.

Similarly, the word "vision" appears 86 times in the Old Testament and 17 in the New Testament, as in the following texts.

- Abraham –Genesis 15
- Jacob –Genesis 46
- Samuel –1 Samuel 3
- Nathan –2 Samuel 7
- Ezekiel –Ezekiel 1, 8, 11, 37 and 43

- Daniel –Daniel 7.
- Peter, James and John –Matthew 17
- Stephen –Acts 7
- Paul – Acts 9; Galatians 1; 2 Corinthians 12.

Of course, we must be realistic, for not every dream and vision is from the Lord. For the enemy, whose purpose is to destroy and cause havoc, will try to lead us astray with false revelations. However, I will say, that this is far less likely, if we are walking before the Lord with a humble and repentant heart. Nevertheless, the Bible does warn us that the enemy "disguises himself as an angel of light" in (2 Corinthians 11:14).

And he can certainly use dreams and visions to bring confusion or to sow seeds of doubt, discouragement and ungodly direction. This is why when we feel like God has given us the interpretation for our dream and vision, that we should confirm it through other reliable and godly sources; as is written in (1 John 4:1), which says, "Believe not every spirit, but try the spirits whether they are of God." And so it is very important to:

1. Test Dreams and Visions Against the Word

Beloved, if a dream or vision tries to persuade you of something contrary to the Word of God, then quite simply it is not from the Lord. For God will never contradict His Word. (1 Peter 1:25) promises this by saying: "the Word of the Lord endures for ever" (KJV). It will never change or become irrelevant, beloved, therefore; we can hold it up as the absolute truth by which we judge all of our dreams and visions.

2. Test Dreams and Visions with Trusted Spiritual-Led Believers

Dreams and visions often confirm what the Spirit of God has already been speaking to the Body of Christ. But having said that, dreams can also be directional or revelatory in nature; as in Paul's case when God was directing him to go to Macedonia; and in the case of Jacob; when he dreamed of the stairway to heaven, and it revealed an aspect of God that Jacob had never really understood before. In addition, God may be trying to get our attention, by sending us a repetitive dream or the dream or vision may stay vividly in our memory for a very long time, as in King Nebuchadnezzar's case. In fact, he was so troubled by his dream, that he called Daniel to interpret it for him, as is confirmed in (Daniel 2:3). But regardless of the type of dream or vision, it is critical to ensure that the message is shared with a trusted, spirit led believer, for messages such as these should not be taken lightly.

In my opinion beloved, dreams and visions will occur more and more frequently in the Body of Christ, in the years ahead, for God wants to lead and direct His people, as we cooperate with Him to bring in the end time harvest of souls into His Kingdom. As you learn to receive these messages and to understand God's purpose in them, I would advise you to do as the Old Testament Prophet, Habakkuk advised in Chapter 2, Verse 2: "Write down the revelation and make it plain on tablets, so that you may run with it." Keep a journal beloved, and reflect and pray over your dreams and visions, and ask for God's guidance, as you learn to walk and grow in this extraordinary gifting. To God be the Glory!

# Chapter 32

## Moving in Prophetic Exploration

Beloved, we are living in the day and hour, that we must be vigilant to press into God, for instructions and then we must endeavour to use keen discernment to ensure we are able to go behind enemy lines and defeat the enemy. The Old Testament speaks about Moses sending out twelve spies in Numbers 13 to explore Canaan, which was given to the Israelites by God. And Moses gave specific instructions of which He had heard from God to these men, as is written in (Numbers 13: 17-20): And when Moses sent these spies to explore Canaan, he told them, "Go through the Negev and then into the mountain region. See what the land is like and whether the people living there are strong or weak, few or many. Is the land they live in good or bad? Do their cities have walls around them or not? Is the soil rich or poor? Does the land have trees or not? Do your best to bring back some fruit from the land."

So, the spies returned 40 days later, and said in verses 27-30: "We went to the land where you sent us. It really is a land flowing with milk and honey. Here's some of its' fruit. But the people who live there are strong, and the cities have walls and are very large. We even saw the descendants of Anak there. The Amalekites live in the Negev. The Hittites, Jebusites, and Amorites live in the mountain region. And the Canaanites live along the coast of the Mediterranean Sea and all along the

Jordan River." Caleb told the people (the other spies) to be quiet and listen to Moses, and Caleb then said, "Let's go now and take possession of the land. We should be more than able to conquer it."

Beloved, when God gives us a directional word, He expects us to submit to Him, and walk in faith to possess the land. Often these words, are quite hard to take in, let alone carry out; but we must remember that God's thoughts and ways, are not our thoughts and ways, as is spoken about in Isaiah 55:8-9: "For my thoughts are not your thoughts, neither are your ways my ways," declares the Lord. As the heavens are higher than the earth, so are my ways higher than your ways, and my thoughts than your thoughts." I can remember a time I was praying in my living room on my own, and God told me that I needed to go to Weid Road (in Houston, Texas); and hold miracle services in a Methodist church there. Now, believe me beloved, the city of Houston is a very large place and I did not have a clue where that road was. But being obedient to God's instruction, I looked on the map and found that it was in North Houston. And so, I called up a wonderful; friend of mine, who is a great prayer warrior and said: "Kathy, the Lord has shown me to go to Weid Road to find a Methodist church to conduct miracle services there; how would you like to do some prophetic exploration?" Well, being as keen as I was, to carry out God's will; Kathy graciously agreed to go with me, and the next day; we set out to find Weid Road.

Beloved, after driving for about an hour, and please bear in mind we didn't have Satnavs back then, we did indeed find Weid Road. It was a narrow, dirt road with a large grove of trees, and I looked at Kathy and said to her, "Well, we have come this far, let's find out if there is anything behind those trees." She gave me an encouraging look and said; "I am believing God with you, that His will shall be carried out, in Jesus name." And we turned left onto that dirt road and slowly drove down it, to see if anything was behind those trees. As we drove past the trees to our great delight, a small and very beautiful little Free Methodist Church came into view." We were both so full of joy when we saw that church that we literally started singing God's praises whilst in the car. Then Kathy said: "it looks like there is a car around the back, why don't you go see if anyone is in there."

I smiled and opened my car door and approached the back door of the church; (as the front doors were locked), and I knocked on the door, feeling both excited and nervous at the same time, and then a young man with wire rimmed spectacles, and in his late twenties; answered the door.

Still feeling nervous; but strongly prompted by the Holy Spirit, I said: "Hello, my name is Leisa, and I am a minister of the gospel of Jesus Christ, and I wondered if we could use your building to conduct miracle services here?" The man looked shocked at my words at first; but then he smiled and replied: "Well, Leisa, I have been praying that the Holy Spirit would begin to work mightily in our church; and I believe God sent you here as an answer to my prayers, so when would you like to start?" He then invited me in and we talked about the details of the miracle services and he also said: "Can you also please come and minister at our church this Sunday; because I want to see a servant of God working under the Power of the Holy Spirit to make a real difference here?"

I felt the Holy Spirit nudging me to accept this assignment, and in that service; and also in all of the miracle services we conducted in that little Methodist church throughout that year, we saw many phenomenal salvations, healings, miracles occur; as a direct result of that young pastor and I, listening to God's voice and stepping out in faith to fulfil His purposes. Beloved, we must be brave, courageous and also, discerning, as we submit to God, and not only hear, but carry out His instructions. People might say "you are crazy," and ridicule you for carrying out God's instructions; but the great healing evangelist, Francis Hunter, once said to a packed church of believers, "I want to know right now, brothers and sisters, are you man pleasers or God pleasers?" "Because I can tell you right now, if you are a God pleaser, then buckle up your seat belts, because it will be exciting and sometimes a rocky ride." I never forgot her words and have certainly experienced both sides of this reality; as I have tried to be obedient in hearing God's voice and carrying out His will.

Beloved, God will require you to sharpen your discernment as you carry out the assignments, He gives you, for the enemy will send distractions and decoys; to try to stop you from doing what God has asked you to do. But God's Word says in (Isaiah 55:11): "So will My Word be, which goes forth from My mouth; It will not return to Me empty, without accomplishing what I desire, And without succeeding in the matter for which I sent it. "

This is only accomplished by communing with God and by pressing in for an intimate relationship with Him each and every day. And only then will you be able to not only recognise His voice when he speaks to you; but also, to feel the power of

His anointing, bolstering your faith; as He prepares you for the work ahead. Then beloved, His secrets will be revealed to you, as it says in (Luke 8:17): 'For there is nothing hidden that will not be disclosed, and nothing concealed that will not be known or brought out into the open. 'Praise God!

# Chapter 33

## Why Do We Need Accountability?

Beloved, as human beings we need to be able to share our victories and our struggles to like-minded people, who have the same goals and outlook as we do. Some say it is to gain perspective, others say it is our way of approaching a problem and gaining a solution. But God's Word says: "that we are best suited to go on life's journey with a companion; and that having two companions can provide an even greater protection from life's many trials.

But remember our primary accountability should always be to God, the Father, as we recognise the great sacrifice His Son, Jesus Christ made to provide us a way of escape from sin and death. In (Mark 6:6–7), we see Jesus sending His disciples out in pairs. Hebrews (10:24–25) encourages believers "… consider how to stir up one another to love and engage in good works, not neglecting to meet together, as is the habit of some, but encouraging one another…"(Ecclesiastes 4:9–12) also says, "Two are better than one, because they have a good reward for their toil. For if they fall, one will lift up his fellow. But woe to him who is alone when he falls and has not another to lift him up!" "Again, if two lie together, they keep warm, but how can one keep warm alone? And though a man might prevail against one who is alone, two will withstand him—a threefold cord is not quickly broken." And beloved, even though this passage in

Ecclesiastes speaks of physical warmth, strength, and assistance when falling down in the natural, it can be applied to the need for spiritual encouragement, strength, and help, as well. In fact, if a friend is seen falling into temptation or sin, Christians are exhorted to correct their brother or sister and help restore them (Galatians 6:1–2).

Similarly, even when a particular sin is not an issue, Christians can still encourage one another to continue walking strong in their faith. The truth is, being accountable to others can help us stand strong in many areas of our Christian walk. But it is important to ensure we are very careful with who we align ourselves with; and such important decisions need to be brought before the Lord in prayer. You see beloved, God does desire, for us to walk in His perfect will; and if we are misaligned in some way with people, who do not share the same values, ethical beliefs and Christian standards; then the enemy can use this dilemma to cause division in the Body of Christ. Beloved, God only wants the best for you, and there are so many benefits in having a spiritual covering over us, as well as brothers and sisters to walk with us, arm in arm. A spiritual covering means when God considers us part of a church or a network of like-minded people; and so, when prayer is lifted up for the people of that church or network; than those that are under their covering, will also reap the blessings of any prayer or declarations that are spoken over that group. Hallelujah! It is very important beloved, that respect and honour is given to pastors and leaders of a ministry, for their burden is great, as their actions can impact the lives of large populations of people in a very significant way.

Beloved, Christians who attempt to walk with God entirely on their own and who do not want to be accountable to other Christian brothers or sisters; can be exposing themselves to a very lonely and trouble filled life, as self-recrimination and self-hatred is almost always the inevitable result. And though it is true that we are ultimately accountable to God, it is also true that in Christ we are part of a family and a body (1 Corinthians 12). With this being the case, we must realise that there really is no such thing as a solo Christian, "turning maverick," for this can certainly open up doors for the enemy to attack us in such a way, that we start to doubt God, as loneliness and desperation sets in. Of course, we all know that challenges will come into our lives (John 16:33); but truly having accountability with other Christians does help us to press forwards with perseverance, despite life's ups and downs Thankfully, an accountability partner can pray with and for us, teach us, rebuke us, rejoice with us, weep with us, and encourage us. And we can do the same for others, as we seek to be a blessing in the Body of Christ. Alleluia!

Once you are truly convinced, that God has called you to the next level and you move forwards in faith, you will begin to feel the responsibility and authority of that level. You will also sense an anointing and a grace from God, to do what you are supposed to be doing in your new season. Praise God!

Beloved, a sincere and humble person accepts and acknowledges what God has done in his or her life. And if you want to live in true humility, do not try to explain away God's work in your life. Instead, be honest about what He is doing, admit your need for His grace and give Him glory at every opportunity and always, always, thank Him for not only what

He has done in your own life, but what He is doing through you to bless others.

Remember, God calls and anoints chosen people for specific roles and tasks; according to His wisdom and grace. And when the time comes for Him to move you to a new level or season, in your life; embrace what He is calling you to do, and feel that release from Him, so that you can now flow in cooperation with God's purposes, without the former limitations barring your way, Amen.

# Chapter 34

## The Serious Role of Prophetic Intercession

As an American prophetic minister, I have planted and pastored three churches over the last 35 years; and I believe that God has relocated me to the UK to help gather the prophets together in the Body of Christ. I also believe that this 'gathering,' must happen in order for these prophets of God to intercede in unity, with revelation and direction, and to worship, and minister in order to help combat the many issues that the enemy is stirring up to cause destruction and spiritual blindness to come upon the United Kingdom and beyond. As such, I have been purposefully pursuing this great mandate, as God opens up doors, and the Lord gave me, this Powerful Prophetic Word to provide me with clarity of His intentions in October 2017.

"My People, I am gathering My Prophets rooted, grounded, and invested in furthering My Kingdom across this land. For I have separated this land from the other European nations to prolong its' usefulness in an effort to bring about a great profiling of the enemy through My Prophets. These prophets will expose his plans and strategies in this season and many seasons to come. This great profiling will enable My People to block the enemy, so that my adversary will no longer attack My Body with weapons of ignorance and superstition. For the great perpetrator Fear, walks as a Spirit, who seeks to blind the eyes and deafen the ears of My People; and even the unsaved, as the winds of revival stir at the gates of the city, London, and other great cities throughout this land. And I am saying beloved, that I will proclaim through My Prophets to the Spirit of Fear, "Let My People Go," so that a new revelation of My power and grace may finally entrench itself in and around My People; and I will then declare the United Kingdom, a strong nation; and the strongholds of terrorism, witchcraft, and sexual sin will be brought down, as My Prophets shout with jubilation and step on the neck of the enemy, trampling him underfoot, says the Lord. And then at last My People will show great compassion and invite the unclean to be cleansed; as my great winds cause all of the uncleanness to be swept away. Beloved, then and only then, will the revival of this land occur in great force, as thousands of Muslims turn from radicalism and come into My Kingdom. And a great loving-kindness will then come upon My People; as they embody My Mercy giving the great unwashed a place of belonging, as sons and daughters, of the Most High God.

Beloved, when God gives direction like this, we must act, because this sort of prophetic word does not only contain an aspirational goal that we hope to achieve someday; so that if we pray hard enough, or act as we should, that somehow, everything will come right in the end. But rather, a prophetic word should give us actual 'Keys to the Kingdom,' as God reveals His mysteries to us through the prophetic ministry. God speaks about the 'Keys to His Kingdom,' in Matthew 16:19, which says: "I will give you the keys of the kingdom of heaven; whatever you bind on earth will be bound in heaven, and whatever you loose on earth will be loosed in heaven."

Beloved, we spoke about what it means to bind the strong man, or the demonic enemy, in your life or the life of others, earlier in this book. But let us look at this verse in the context of a prophetic word, when God brings forth strategy and direction. You see, when such a word is brought forth by a prophetic minister, both the heavens and the earth begin to shake, for as we, His people; intercede and begin to act upon that rhema word, in obedience to God's direction, a powerful God given force is loosed upon the earth and each demonic door is unlocked and the captives are then set free. Hallelujah!

During my many years as a prophetic minister, I have seen and heard countless powerful prophetic words; but sadly, many times these words are not really honoured or taken seriously in church services or other ministry events. In fact, many of them are only interpreted as being inspirational or symbolic at best, rather than the tangible and life-giving strategies that God has really intended them to be. Beloved, in the times we are now living in, with the scale of immorality and violence upon the earth, we need to "smarten up" and realise our need to hear from God at every opportunity, on how to deal with these terrible dilemmas that face our generation and many generations to come. And whilst I agree that such words must align with the Word of God and be confirmed by two or more witnesses. We cannot afford to turn a deaf ear to those with prophetic giftings, for believe me, I myself have often delivered such words at a great cost to my physical health and reputation; because I wanted at all times to be obedient to God's voice. And most true prophetic ministers stand humbly before God delivering such messages, not really knowing how they will be received by their brothers and sisters in Christ.

In (1 Samuel 15:22), it says: "But Samuel replied: "Does the LORD delight in burnt offerings and sacrifices as much as in obeying the LORD? To obey is better than sacrifice, and to heed is better than the fat of rams." Beloved, obedience is an important key to God's Kingdom that unlocks the life-giving Power of God into our circumstances. For it is without question, the response of someone who is in a trust relationship with God. And this act of faith demonstrates to God that we totally and completely depend on Him for our breakthrough. This also shows God we have a listening ear to His instructions; and as we interact with Him, our closeness to our Father, God; causes victory in every area of our lives. You see, obedience is better than sacrifice; because we are letting God be God and staying in our proper place in cooperation with Him. Which is the place of dependence and surrender to His Mercy, Wisdom, and Power, as He helps us to defeat the enemy and learn to walk in His freedom and His truth.

# Chapter 35

## Understanding Destiny

Destiny is an important concept that Christians must fully understand to be able to fulfil the Perfect Will of God in their lives. Sadly, because of unrepentant sin conditions and people's disobedience, there are often hindrances in achieving God's Perfect Will; which can in turn, open doors to demonic strongholds, either delaying or blocking altogether God's plans for our lives. Consequently, a generational blessing of "walking in the fulfilment of God's true destiny for our lives", can move on to the next generation; and if they also continue to disobey, then it may even skip several generations, until a person actually follows after God with their whole heart. Now I am not saying, "that a person is unsaved, when this occurs, for only God can be the true judge of that," but I am saying that many of us may not walk in the true power and freedom that God has intended for us, and will miss out on our true destiny; because of a continued cycle of varied sin conditions. Remember beloved, there are three states of being that exist for a Christian, when we are talking about destiny; and that is God's Perfect Will, God's Permissive Will, and a 'Failure to Thrive,' Existence. God's Perfect Will for our lives is achieved by walking in obedience to the principle spoken of in (Romans 12:2), which says: "Do not be conformed to this present world, but be transformed by the renewing of your mind, so that you may test and approve what is the will of God-what is good and well-pleasing and perfect." Beloved, to truly know your purpose on this earth and to be able to fulfil your destiny you must spend intimate times communing with God, and letting His glory and grace renew your mind. In addition, learning His precepts in the Bible will help you to understand the very character and nature of God; so that you can be like Him, and personify His ways, in everything you do. These two key actions will not only help you to be led of the Holy Spirit; but also, to hear His voice and cooperate with Him when He asks you to do something.

There is also what we might call God's "permissive will." In other words, when we end up taking "the scenic route," and taking ten times longer to learn something; because of spiritual blindness or pride, which is rooted in a sin condition. This is what God allows, even though it is sin. A good example, is when God allowed Joseph's brothers to betray him, and to deceive their father, so that He might bring the Israelites (few in number) to Egypt, where God would spare them, and they would greatly multiply (Genesis 50:20). You see beloved, God allows man to reject the gospel, to wilfully disobey His laws, to persecute the righteous, and so on, when perhaps in the end, His Perfect Will can be accomplished. Remember God loves us so much, and if there is a praying family member, He will often allow things to occur in order to bring answers to that prayer. This "Grace from God" allows time and circumstances for our loved ones or indeed ourselves, to truly understand about our dire circumstances and the need to repent, and at last turn to Him. God is Sovereign and can be creative in His ways; as long as His purposes are being accomplished. Hallelujah!

A "Failure to Thrive" state is when an individual goes into what I call a sort of spiritual shock or "survival mode." And again, I am not here to say that these people in this category "are unsaved," but I can without question say, "that these people are not living victorious lives." Usually these types people, do not grow into spiritual maturity and stay in a place of woundedness and lack of understanding for the whole of their lives, which makes living their lives extremely difficult most of the time. This is described in (1 Corinthians 3:1-5), where it says: "Brothers, I could not address you as spiritual, but as worldly -- mere infants in Christ. I gave you milk, not solid food, for you were not yet ready for it. Indeed, you are still not ready. You are still worldly. For since there is jealousy and quarrelling among you, are you not worldly? Are you not acting like mere men? For when one says, "I follow Paul," and another, "I follow Apollos," are you not mere men?"

In the world, the exact polar opposite to God's teachings on fulfilling our destiny, is fatalism. Fatalism is a major premise of Islam, which demands "total submission" to the sovereignty of Allah. It is widely held in Hinduism, too; in fact, it is a fatalistic view of life that helps keep India's caste system in place and causes horrific oppression and terrorism to take place around the world. Greek mythology told of the Moirai, or the Fates, where three goddesses were pictured as weavers of men's lives. Their decisions could not be cancelled or annulled, even by other gods. Fatalism is "absolutely not a Biblical concept." Thankfully, the Bible teaches that Man was created with the ability to make moral choices, and that he is responsible for those choices. The Fall of Man was not a predetermined event in which Adam and Eve were hapless victims of a Puppet-Master God. On the contrary, Adam and his wife had the ability to choose obedience (with all of its' wonderful blessing) or disobedience (with its' terrible curse). They knew what the result of their decision would be, and they were held accountable, as is written about in Genesis 3. This theme of being held accountable for our choices continues throughout Scripture. "He who sows wickedness reaps trouble" (Proverbs 22:8). "All hard work brings a profit, but mere talk leads only to poverty" (Proverbs 14:23). "Do you want to be free from fear of the one in authority? Then do what is right and he will commend you" (Romans 13:3).

And often beloved, when the Bible speaks of destiny, it's in reference to a destiny people have brought upon themselves: "Many live as enemies of the Cross of Christ." This its written about in (Philippians 3:18-19): "Their destiny is destruction." (Psalm 49:13), says: "This is the fate of those who trust in themselves;" (Proverbs 6:32), says: "A man who commits adultery lacks judgment; whoever does so destroys himself," and (Revelations 20:13), further says: "Each person was judged according to what he had done."

The facts are, that we sin because we choose to. We can't blame "Fate," kismet, predestination, or God, as is written in. (James 1:13-14), which says: "When tempted, no one should say, 'God is tempting me.' For God cannot be tempted by evil, nor does he tempt anyone; but each one is tempted when, by his own evil desire, he is dragged away and enticed." Interestingly, many people who choose to sin, are annoyed by the negative consequences of their sin. This is spoken about in (Proverbs 19:3), which says: "A man's own folly ruins his life, yet, his heart rages against the LORD." This is a very thought-provoking verse. In other words, when a man foolishly wrecks his life, he may still insist on blaming God, or perhaps "Fate." In this way, he persists in his folly. Scripture also teaches that we have to choose to have faith. This often-repeated command in the Bible, "to believe," seems to imply that we do have a choice in the matter, as is written in (John 20:27): "Be not faithless, but believing, "and in additional scriptures in (Acts 16:31; and 19:4). It is important beloved, that we do not get the wrong idea, and believe that "we are the captains of our own destiny," for this is simply not true. Only God is sovereign. His sovereign control is called "providence." And He has chosen to give us a free will, and He has created a moral universe in which the law of cause-and-effect is an absolute reality. But remember that God is God alone, and there are no "accidents" in the universe. None at all.

He is a God with manifold wisdom and power and He most definitely has a plan, and so it should be of no surprise to us, that the Bible speaks of a divine plan. In fact, God's plan for our destiny. The destiny that God is working to bring about for all of His creation, is spoken about in (Isaiah 48:3), "I foretold the former things long ago, my mouth announced them and I made them known; then suddenly I acted, and they came to pass." Beloved, what God decrees, He does (and He may decree or announce it, centuries ahead of time!). My friend, fighting against the plan of God is pointless. This is confirmed in (Proverbs 21:30), where it says: "There is no wisdom, no insight, no plan, that can succeed against the LORD." This is why the Tower of Babel was never completed, as spoken about in (Genesis 11:1-9); and why Daniel's enemies were thrown to the lions, as spoken about in (Daniel 6:24). This is also why

Jonah spent time inside a fish, as spoken about in (Jonah 1:17); and why all of us cause trouble for ourselves, when we sin and veer off God's plan for our lives. Even what we would normally call "chance" or "fate" is under God's control. This is proven in (Proverbs 16:33), which says: "The lot is cast into the lap, but its' every decision is from the LORD."

In other words, God does not take a "hands-off" approach to running the world. God's sovereignty reaches even to a plan for our individual lives. This is illustrated in God's calling of Jeremiah—before the prophet was even born, as is written in (Jeremiah 1:4-5): "The word of the LORD came to me, saying, 'Before I formed you in the womb I knew you, before you were born I set you apart; I appointed you as a prophet to the nations'." David also recognized that the Lord had a plan for him, when he said in (Psalm 139:16): "Your eyes saw my unformed body. All the days ordained for me were written in your book before one of them came to be." And because of this knowledge, David sought the Lord's specific guidance in many situations, such as in (1 Samuel 23:9-12). In (Acts 9), Jesus appears to Saul of Tarsus with an interesting statement: "It is hard for you to kick against the goads" (verse 5). Jesus obviously had a plan for Saul, and Saul had been (painfully) resisting it. You can believe it beloved that exercising our freedom against God's plan can be painful. (I have definitely walked down that road a time or two.) Later, Jesus tells Saul that a man named Ananias would come to visit —and then Jesus tells Ananias (verses 11-12)! Obviously, Jesus had a pre-arranged plan for Ananias as well. Now, Ananias didn't want to visit Saul (verse 13-14). He could have been like Jonah and run the other way. If that had been his choice, God would have had a "fish" prepared to bring him back. Fortunately, Ananias obeyed God's plan (verse 17). And proved that exercising our freedom to follow God's plan brings a blessing.

In summary, the Bible teaches that God is in charge. At the same time, He has given us the freedom to obey or disobey Him, and there are some things that God does only in answer to prayer (James 4:2). God blesses the obedient, and He is patient with those who disobey, even to the point of the seems like the 9$^{th}$ hour at times. But reassuringly, He has a plan for our lives, which includes both our fulfilment and His glory both in this world and in the world to come. Thankfully, those who have accepted Jesus Christ as their Saviour; have accepted God's plan, as is written about in (John 14:6). From then on, it's a step-by-step process of learning to live in the calling and destiny that God, our Father, has meant for us all along. Hallelujah!

L - #0226 - 170220 - C0 - 210/148/12 - PB - DID2770834